CAS Paper 4

'ɔɔɔ7(42) coɐ.

# The economy of upland Britain, 1750-1950: an illustrated review

E J T Collins

Centre for Agricultural Strategy
University of Reading
Earley Gate
Reading  RG6 2AT

May 1978

ISBN 0 7049 0606 6
ISSN    0141 1330

Printed at the College of Estate Management, Reading

The Centre for Agricultural Strategy was established by the Nuffield Foundation on the campus of the University of Reading in October 1975

# Preface

In September 1977 the Centre, in conjunction with the Department of Agriculture and Horticulture, University of Reading held a symposium entitled *The Future of Upland Britain*. The Centre asked Dr E J T Collins of the Institute of Agricultural History, University of Reading to present an introductory paper to the symposium outlining some of the more important historical aspects of Upland Britain. Such was the interest shown in Dr Collins' paper and in the exhibition of photographs prepared by Mrs H J Woolley of the Museum of English Rural Life, University of Reading, the Centre decided to publish these together with some statistical data collected during the preparation of the paper.

The paper shows the part the uplands played in the Industrial Revolution by providing food, materials, manufactured goods and manpower for the expanding industries of the lowlands. It shows also how the upland economy was able to support a once larger population and why, after 1880, this economy began to decline.

The Centre wishes to thank Dr Collins and Mrs Woolley for their contributions. The photographs are acknowledged as follows:

Museum of English Rural Life, University of Reading, 33, 34, 36, 39, 44, 46, 50; National Museum of Antiquities of Scotland, Country Life Section, Edinburgh, 32, 35, 38, 40, 42, 48, 49, 55, 58, 59, 60, 61; National Museum of Wales, Department of Industry, Cardiff, 51, 52, 53, 54, 56, 57; Welsh National Folk Museum, St Fagans, Cardiff, 37, 41, 43, 45, 47, 62, 63, 64, 65, 66, 67, 68.

# Contents

Appendices I — V

Some statistical information on the economy of upland Britain, 1750-1950, compiled by R B Tranter

Appendix I: The population of upland Britain, 1801-1951

Appendix II: The land use of upland Britain, 1790-1950

## ABBREVIATIONS

HIDB     Highlands and Islands Development Board
MW        Megawatt
MAFF     Ministry of Agriculture, Fisheries and Food


## METRIC EQUIVALENTS

1 acre     = 0.4046 hectares
1 foot     = 0.3048 metres
1 gallon   = 4.5461 litres
1 mile     = 1.6093 kilometres
1 ounce   = 28.350 grams
1 ton      = 1.0161 tonnes

## INTRODUCTION

In 1700 Scotland was a *terra incognita* to the majority of lowland English and was even supposed by some Europeans to be a separate island. Daniel Defoe, who visited the remoter parts of Britain in the early-18th century, described the Scottish Highlands as "a frightful country full of hidious dasart mountains and unpassable", and parts of Wales as, "so like the Alps, that except the language of the people, one could hardly avoid thinking he is passing from Grenoble to Susa . ." (Defoe, 1962 edition). But despite its remoteness the upland zone was then in fact less barbaric and more economically developed than is commonly supposed. By 1700 many parts were already linked to the lowland zone through the sheep and cattle trade and in a few areas non-ferrous mining was already well-established.

The modern economic history of the uplands[1] is dominated by two factors; first, the spread and backwash effects of the Industrial and Agricultural Revolutions on the hinterland economy; and second, the harsh physical environment which meant not only that upland agriculture was much less productive than in other regions but that alternative economic opportunities had to be sought out and and exploited in order to secure the same high levels of income and employment as in the lowland zone. The Industrial Revolution was of vital impact. In the long run it caused the upland economy to decline, but for a while, until the third quarter of the 19th century, it stimulated economic growth. Some areas such as the hill districts of the West Riding, Flint and Denbigh and the Welsh coal valleys were drawn into the mainstream of the British economy, and prospered. But in other areas, such as the Scottish Highlands, where the resource base was thin and the capacity for economic growth therefore strictly limited, the 'backwash effects'

1   This paper is concerned primarily with the upland parts of Scotland (including Aberdeen and Perthshire), upland Wales and upland Northern England.

of the Industrial and Agricultural Revolutions were already apparent by the late-18th century. Yet directly or indirectly all regions in the upland zone played a part in the Industrial Revolution; as producers of food, mineral ores or manufactured goods; or as sources of manpower for the expanding industries of the lowland zone.

## Table 1
## POPULATION TRENDS IN UPLAND BRITAIN, 1801-1951 (thousands)

|  | 1801 | 1841 | 1881 | 1921 | 1951 |
|---|---|---|---|---|---|
| Cumberland and Westmorland | 158 | 234 | 315 | 339 | 352 |
| Remainder of upland England[1] | 1 228 | 2 244 | 4 341 | 6 660 | 7 199 |
| ALL ENGLAND | 8 352 | 15 003 | 24 613 | 35 679 | 41 584 |
| Flint and Denbigh | 99 | 155 | 193 | 265 | 316 |
| Remainder of upland Wales[1] | 281 | 446 | 514 | 545 | 513 |
| ALL WALES | 541 | 911 | 1 361 | 2 208 | 2 174 |
| Upland Scotland[1] | 595 | 757 | 776 | 702 | 646 |
| ALL SCOTLAND | 1 608 | 2 620 | 3 736 | 4 882 | 5 096 |

1   For delineation see Appendix I.

Source: Appendix I.

## Table 2
## DATES WHEN MAXIMUM POPULATIONS FIRST REACHED IN UPLAND BRITAIN, 1831-1931

| | Number of counties recording maximum populations in census years: | | | | | | | | | | |
|---|---|---|---|---|---|---|---|---|---|---|---|
| | 1831 | 1841 | 1851 | 1861 | 1871 | 1881 | 1891 | 1901 | 1911 | 1921 | 1931 |
| Upland England[1] | — | — | — | — | — | — | 1 | — | — | 1 | 5 |
| Upland Wales[1] | 1 | 1 | — | 1 | 2 | — | — | — | — | 2 | 2 |
| Upland Scotland[1] | 3 | 1 | 2 | 3 | — | 2 | — | 1 | — | — | — |

1   For delineation see Appendix I.

Source: See Appendix I.

The outstanding historical fact of modern times is that over much of the upland zone the population is now smaller than a century ago. In parts of the

Scottish Highlands it declined before 1800 and four Scottish counties recorded their maximum populations before 1850. (See Table 2). But even where the population continued to expand, in many of the poorer agricultural districts it was already declining in or before the mid-19th century. There were striking differences between demographic trends in the different regions, depopulation occuring sooner in Scotland than in Wales, for example. (See Tables 1 and 2). The trend was determined partly by the push factors of population pressure, land hunger, under-employment, and the decline of non-agricultural industry, but more by the pull of higher wages and better living standards in the lowlands where employment increased dramatically after 1830. Progressively the geographical balance of economic activity and of population tilted in favour of the lowlands. The upland zone (excepting the industrial counties of northern England) contained less than 5% of the national population in 1950 as against 15-20% in the mid-18th century. In Scotland, in 1755, over half of the population lived north of the Tay compared with 20% in 1900. In Wales the share of the population living in the industrial counties of Monmouth and Glamorgan grew from less than 20% in 1800 to more than 60% in 1950. (See also Appendix I for more detailed statistical data on population trends.)

The Highlands and Islands of Scotland were regarded as a 'depressed area' in the 18th century, but other upland areas were recognised officially as such only after the 1930's. The so-called 'hill farm problem' is a modern invention which was not properly identified until the agricultural advisory provinces were established, although some work had been done on the productivity of hill sheep farming by the Food Production Department in 1918. Indeed, hill farms were often thought to be more depression-proof than lowland farms because of the greater resilience of livestock farming during the periods of falling prices, and lower labour costs. In 1913, Daniel Hall said of Cardiganshire: " . . . the people seemed cheerful and prosperous, the market was animated, and there was no sign of economic pressure to force a higher standard of farming" (Hall, 1913). In the 1930's, however, attention was focused on the economically depressed regions of the north and west, and on the hill farmer. In 1936, Sir George Stapledon proposed an ambitious scheme of wasteland improvement in the hill districts of Wales, which, he argued, would not only create employment but also help maintain a virile Welsh hill population whose genius and enterprise would otherwise, like the silt of the mountain streams, have flowed down to invigorate the lowlands (Stapledon, 1936). There was a call also for a programme of agricultural reconstruction aimed at increasing national self-sufficiency, especially in livestock foods, and reversing the process whereby, "For generations past industry has been slow denuding the countryside of its more vigorous human strains" (Astor & Rowntree, 1938).

Since the Second World War, the 'upland problem' has been more precisely defined and made more urgent by the demands of Celtic nationalists for greater regional equality. At the same time, the Keynesian revolution in economic thinking has given political as well as intellectual respectability to the efforts by government to redistribute income and investment between the regions. But as an historical process the problem is by no means fully understood. A regional economy is, almost by definition, an open economy, which means that the pattern of development in the past was determined by movements in relative factor costs, terms of trade and balance of comparative advantage. The economic history of the upland zone, therefore, is reflective of changes in the structure of the national economy and in the pattern of international trade.

The next section will examine why and by what combination of resources the upland economy was able to support the once larger population, and why during and after the late-19th century, the upland economy lost most of its earlier vigour.

AGRICULTURE IN THE UPLAND ECONOMY, 1750-1880

Between 1750 and 1850, upland agriculture was able to absorb only a part of the population increase. Most of the Scottish Highlands were already over-populated in relation to agricultural resources before the mid-18th century and suffered acutely during the famine years 1693-1700 (The 'Seven Ill Years'), 1709 and 1740-1746, when sometimes whole families died of starvation and cattle were fed on whins and broom for want of sufficient grass. The constraints on higher output, then as now, were the poor prospects of arable farming (limited to lower altitudes), and the sterility of upland pastures. Upland farmers were unable to exploit new technical developments, notably the turnip and leguminous fodder crops, which were the basis of the Agricultural Revolution in the lowlands. The dream of every improving landlord with a fortune to spend was to introduce mixed farming into the uplands, thereby to break the fodder-bottleneck and set in motion the virtuous cycle of crop, stock and farmyard dung. Between 1871 and 1892, the Duke of Sutherland spent £254 000 enclosing the outrun and reclaiming 2643 acres of poor moorland at Strath Terry on the shores of Loch Shin. Sixteen sets of steam tackle were at work in 1875 but, though the original intention was to cultivate oats and root crops, most of the arable reverted to grass after 1880. On Exmoor large tracts of the Forest were reclaimed and enclosed between 1820 and the 1860's, but here also, the system of sheep and corn-growing (based on the Norfolk Four Course system) was abandoned in the higher parts after 1840.

Agricultural output in the uplands increased in response to population growth and rising prices. Higher output was secured at both margins; intensively, by the use of lime which was the cheapest and most effective means of improving acidic moorland pasture, and by the cultivation of potatoes which became a mainstay of the cottage diet; extensively, by reclamation. Population pressure on the better land led to the sub-division of smaller farms and forced the margin of cultivation up the hillsides onto the less fertile soils. In the Yorkshire Dales, Dartmoor and elsewhere, the task of farming the waste was left to small farmers who reclaimed it piece by piece, thus serrating the moorland fringe with a patchwork of new enclosures.

The most important agricultural enterprise of the upland zone remained, as before, the breeding and rearing of young stock for sale to lowland graziers. In the Scottish Highlands sheep replaced black cattle as the chief store animal following the discovery there, in the mid-18th century, that sheep could be successfully outwintered. The subsequent rapid increase in the Highland sheep population, from less than 500 000 in the 1750's to more than 2.5 million in the 1870's, is associated with the notorious 'Highland Clearances' (see Table III.6). While it is true that some native tenants were evicted, brutish landlords were only one factor in the depopulation of the Highlands. The breakdown of the old clan system was another: for it had held people to the region and kept the population artificially high; when it disintegrated the trickle of out-migration became a flood, especially after 1790 when industry began rapidly to expand in the Central Lowlands and during the Napoleonic Wars when large numbers of Highlanders joined the army.

Throughout the upland zone sheep farming was the predominant enterprise. The hill flocks grew and multiplied and their quality was improved by the infusion of new and better blood into the traditional breeds and by the introduction of new types. Agricultural output rose but in peasant farming agricultural output per capita rose only very slightly, if at all before 1850, and as the number of dependants increased so their marginal productivity declined. Under-employment forced many of them to move away, to take up by-employments, or migrate each summer to the lowlands to work in the harvest fields, in construction or in the fishing industry. In many districts seasonal migration was an integral part of the small-farm economy and kept it afloat.

The most impressive improvements in output and productivity tended to occur near large centres of population, in the busier mining districts or around the industrial towns where there was a buoyant market for meat, milk, vegetables and hay. A French agriculturist who visited Wales in the 1850's, said of it, that whereas elsewhere such a country would be "almost deserted by man", the working of mines and quarries had caused "a disproportionate agricultural development" (de Lauvergne, 1855). The correlation between proximity to industrial markets and land use was especially apparent on the upland fringe overlooking the coalfields.

# EXTRACTIVE INDUSTRIES IN THE UPLAND ECONOMY, 1750-1880

Distance and high transport costs could be insuperable obstacles to industrial development in the upland zone but there occurred some striking improvements in communications after 1750. In northern Scotland, the Crinian Canal, dissecting the Mull of Kintyre, was opened in 1801, and the Caledonian Canal, linking Loch Linnhe and the Moray Firth, in 1822. The dense canal networks of northern England, crossing the Peak District and southern Pennines, and the canal system of the West Midlands, extending as far as Newtown and Llangollen, were built between 1770 and 1810, to the benefit of mine-owners and manufacturers on the upland fringe. The 18th and early-19th centuries also saw many road improvements which speeded-up journey times and permitted a wider intercourse which in many areas had hitherto been reserved for drovers. The first road in the Shetlands was constructed in 1781 while by the 1820's, in the wake of the new turnpike roads, stage coaches were running between Edinburgh and Inverness.

It was thought at the time that the Industrial Revolution would entirely transform the upland economy. It did so in Derbyshire and the West Riding and in the coal valleys of South Wales, but in that 'age of miracles' the spirit of optimism pervaded even the Scottish Highlands. Daniel Defoe who visited northern Scotland in 1707, said of the region: "Some people tell us they have both lead, copper and iron in this part of Scotland and I am much inclined to believe it: but it seems reserved for a future and more industrious age to search into ... And should a time ever come when these hidden treasures of the earth should be discover'd and improv'd, this part of Scotland may no longer be call'd poor, for such a production would soon change the face of things, bring wealth and people and commerce to it; fill their harbours full of ships; their towns full of people; and by consuming the provisions, bring the soil to be cultivated, its fish cur'd, and its cattel consum'd at home" (Defoe, 1962 edition).

The prospect of mineral wealth, of *copiae sub terra*, had excited the imagination of lowland capitalists since the time of the Romans. They discovered, of course, that not every mountain was 'God's Treasure House', but non-ferrous ores were widely distributed throughout the upland zone and often in insufficient qualities to support a mining industry. It is not generally realised, that as late as 1850 over half the world's production of copper, zinc, lead, and tin was derived from British ores, mainly from upland Britain. Even gold was discovered in commercial quantities, in Merioneth in the 1840's and Sutherland in the 1860's. The Highlands and Islands though, were found to have few workable deposits apart from some copper in Islay and Shetland and lead at Strontian and Tyndrum, but not before considerable sums of money had been lost chasing the illusion of great lodes of copper wherever green staining appeared on the surface. During the Industrial Revolution, regional development in the upland zone was very much influenced by the fact that the pre-Cambrian rocks of the Scottish Highlands were much less productive of metallic ores than the younger rocks of Wales and the Pennines.

Some mines, such as the copper mine at Parys Mountain in Anglesey, and a few Cornish tin and Welsh lead mines were large concerns employing hundreds of workers, but most mines were very small, comprising a few shafts or adits, owned and in many cases worked by local farmers and tradesmen. In north Cardigan alone there were over 100 recorded lead mines, and in Flint and Denbigh over 150, of which only a handful ever produced more than 100 tons of dressed ore in a single year. The larger mines, whilst more productive, were also more costly and required large injections of speculative capital for site and drainage works and the purchase of plant.

In addition to metals, some areas, notably Merioneth, Caernarvon and Aberdeen, had important slate and stone industries. The demand for Welsh slates rose after the repeal of the slate tax in 1831; output at Ffestiniog, the main centre of the industry, rose nearly ten times between 1831 and 1878, and its population increased six times. According to the 1851 Census, 13% of the male workforce of North Wales was then employed in mining and quarrying. In fact, the proportion was probably much higher because large numbers of workmen, mine-owners as well as wage-earners, were enumerated under agricultural headings as 'farmers', 'farmers' relatives', and 'agricultural labourers'. Mining and agriculture were interdependent, and the expansion of the one often stimulated the other. In the lead mining district of Wanlockhead in Dumfries, for example, the miners were said to have reclaimed a considerable amount of hill-land 'so as to yield hay for their cows . . .'.

The upland zone was deficient in both coal and iron ore, but for a short while during the 17th and 18th centuries, when wood was a prime source of fuel, it supported a charcoal-iron industry. After 1700, English iron-masters, already well established in the hills of Brecon and Monmouth, and in Furness, began to look further afield for supplies of wood. In 1715 the Shropshire ironmaster, Abraham Darby, was operating a works near Cader Idris in Snowdonia, and between 1725 and 1775 furnaces were erected at several places in the Western Highlands of Scotland where local charcoal, blown by water-driven bellows, was used to smelt iron ore imported by sea from Cumberland and Lancashire. The industry had virtually disappeared by 1800 following the invention of the coke-smelting process which drew the iron industry down to the coalfields. (See Appendix V for mineral deposits.)

## MANUFACTURING, FISHING AND FORESTRY IN THE UPLAND ECONOMY, 1750-1880

The agricultural economy of the upland zone was a perfect niche for domestic industry using family labour and local raw materials. It gave employment in the slack periods of the farming year and thus provided extra income at little or no opportunity cost. In many parts of Wales, Cumbria and the Pennines there was already a thriving export trade in hand-made textiles before 1700. The pace of cottage industrialisation quickened after 1750 but the turning point occurred around 1780 following the invention of new forms of textile machinery. In this, the first stage of the Industrial Revolution, the swift-flowing mountain streams spelt cheap water-power and textile manufacturers were soon moving up the valleys in search of suitable sites. The advantage of the early wool-textile machines was their relative cheapness, so that not only capitalist producers but also farmers and local businessmen could erect them. After 1830 most of the cottage looms and spinning wheels and many of the smaller mills were destroyed by factory competition but, as late as 1895, there were several hundred establishments making flannel, shirts and blankets in West Wales. Hand-textile industries were founded in the Scottish Islands in the 18th century and by the 1840's a considerable trade in tweeds and knitted stockings had been developed.

Among the smaller manufacturing industries, 'kelp-making' and distilling were locally important in the Highlands and Islands. 'Kelp' or sea-weed ash was a valuable source of potash, soda and iodine, and 'kelp-burning' was a major activity on the coasts from 1750 to the 1820's. The distilling of malt whisky was traditionally the small-scale enterprise, often illicit, of small farmers. Malt whisky had a wide market in the 18th century and in the 1820's when duties were reduced, the era of the 'whisky lairds' began.

Among the other extractive industries fishing was by far the most important, especially in Scotland where it had a wide distribution. In the 18th and 19th centuries fishing in Scotland was actively encouraged by the State and by local landowners. It became a main support of the crofting community although in terms of output it was soon over-shadowed by the more rapidly expanding fisheries of the east coast. Yet, so great was its importance that, in 1891, 75% of the whole population of the Highlands and Islands were said to be directly or indirectly dependent on it. Salmon fishing was locally important in the river estuaries of West Wales and North-East Scotland. In the 1860's it was said to employ some 400 men, mostly small farmers, in the Tywi Valley alone.

Forestry, however, was a poor provider and except for a few areas like the Upper Spey, Deeside, the Great Glen, and parts of Perthshire, there was little creative interest in it before the mid-19th century. In 1845 there were fewer than 150 000 acres of woodland in the Highlands and Islands, and in the counties of Caithness and Sutherland only 6800 acres. Apart from a passing spell around 1800 when high bark prices gave an impetus to the production of oak coppice, woodlands were of secondary importance to sheep farming, and diminished as a result. The coppice and underwood trades were important in Lakeland, Furness and the Usk and Wye Valleys where, by the mid-19th century, large numbers were employed making poles, tool handles, bobbins, and barrel hoops for export to other areas.

## THE DECLINE OF UPLAND INDUSTRY AFTER 1880

The third quarter of the 19th century was a watershed in the modern economic history of the upland zone. Thereafter the tide of prosperity turned and rapidly ebbed. Thus were dashed the hopes that the coming of the railways would remove the last great obstacle to economic progress and that a few short bounds would bring the uplands level with other more industrialised regions. The industries of the upland zone wilted because in a free trade economy they could not compete with producers in the lowlands and overseas who enjoyed an increasing comparative advantage in terms of markets, natural resources and returns to scale. Some branches of manufacturing industry, such as textiles, began to wilt in the 1830's, but the decline became more general after 1880 when the world price of food and raw materials began to fall and the pace of competition in manufactured goods began to quicken. Before the 1870's, Britain was not seriously threatened by foreign competition, and high levels of output at the margin — in the little mines and factories and windswept fields of the upland zone — were sustained by high prices. But whereas subsequently, in the late-19th century, other countries protected their industries, Britain pursued a policy of free trade, and agriculture and non-ferrous mining — the corner-stones of the upland economy — were exposed to the full blast of foreign competition. In the early-18th century the upland zone had been comparatively well-resourced in respect of water-power, mineral deposits and even land, but by 1880 their productive potential was exhausted and, when these failed, the least efficient producers went under.

Other factors also threatened the survival of manufacturing industry in the upland zone. One was the backwash effect of technical progress in other regions which, in the second stage of the Industrial Revolution, took a large and increasing toll of marginal producers. After 1830 manufacturing industry in Britain became more concentrated in and around the ports and coalfields. The prospects of upland industry began to recede as coal became increasingly the predominant energy source and as the size of firms and scale of technology increased. Also the implications of the geological accident which had denied the upland zone any large deposits of coal and iron-ore gradually became clear. Moreover, the railways mainly benefited lowland producers and tended rather to widen the gap in distribution costs between the inner and outer regions.

Thus, the mobile factors of production — capital, labour and entrepreneurship — migrated from the uplands downhill to other regions. Capital-intensive industry was established only where it enjoyed a unique advantage, as for example in slate or stone. Industrial establishments, where they survived, were small and badly equipped. Nor did the coming of electricity, the oil engine and the motor lorry, significantly alter the picture, because by then, in the last and most recent stage of the Industrial Revolution, the object of enterprise had shifted from capital goods and raw materials to consumer goods. Between the wars industrial investment was focussed more than ever on the lowland zone, on London and the Midlands, while the traditional industries — coal, iron and textiles — were acutely depressed. In the age of mass consumption, the remote and thinly populated upland zone had few attractions. As its industrial base contracted, so its economy became more open and more peripheral.

The prospects for manufacturing industry were the more bleak because earlier in the Industrial Revolution neither textiles, nor mining, nor even agriculture had generated the backward and forward linkages which were a necessary part of the infrastructure of a mature, broadly-based economy. Most of the more advanced mining and textile machinery, as well as agricultural machinery, was imported from other regions. In the same way, most mineral ores were smelted at the coalfields or the ports, in South Wales and South Lancashire, while most of the metal-working was done around Birmingham, London and Bristol.

After 1880, one after the other, the upland industries slid into decay. Non-ferrous mining began to slide following the fall in ore prices in 1878. Between 1885 and 1909-1913 copper-ore production in Britain fell by 86%, tin-ore by 45%, zinc- and lead-ore each by 47%, and all fell even further between the wars. There was a temporary revival in the late 1930's and during the Second World War, but in 1970 there were no active copper, zinc or lead mines, in the country, and only three working tin mines. Mining was affected not only by foreign competition but also by the exhaustion of its raw material. The smallness of the deposits, their geological complexity and unpredictable yields, discouraged investment in modern plant and machinery. The same ore bodies that had repaid extraction in the 1870's were passed over, and existing mines, many of which had been marginal even in prosperous times, were gradually abandoned. Stone and slate held out longer but they too declined after 1920 in the face of increasing competition from other building materials — steel, concrete, tarmacadam and clay and concrete tiles. Slate production in the late 1930's was only half that in 1912.

Manufacturing industry fared little better. Many textile mills had already closed before 1870. The West Wales woollen industry flagged in the 1880's and declined sharply after 1920. The tweed and knit-wear trades in Shetland and the Outer Hebrides alone survived the depression, but the other great Highland industry, distilling, lost ground between the wars with the number of working plants falling from 112 in 1917 to 35 in the mid-1930's. Elsewhere, in Monmouth and Furness, the coppice and underwood industries had virtually disappeared by the time of the First World War. The Scottish fishing industry flourished until 1920 when, following the loss of European export markets, it too became enfeebled, although the position of the crofter-fishermen had already been undermined as a result of the concentration of the industry at the East-coast ports, and by the introduction of steam drifters and steam trawlers which outfished and outdistanced the smaller boats and decimated the inshore fishing grounds. In 1938 fishing gave employment to only 13 400 people in the Highlands compared with over 30 000 at the turn of the century. The gutting and packing of fish had been a main seasonal employment for Highland women and its decline was severely felt by the crofting community for whom fishing, in its various forms, had been a larger source of income than agriculture (see Tables I.8 and I.9 for examples of changes in the industrial distribution of the labour force in this period).

## UPLAND AGRICULTURE, 1880-1950

The present day problems of the upland zone reflect the failure to reconstruct the economy and to introduce industries which generated income and employment on a sufficient scale to stem the tide of rural migration. One response was to intensify agricultural production. But where this was done the farming population steadily declined although that was to the benefit of those who remained and whose real incomes improved. Agricultural performance was mixed. Tillage declined nearly everywhere but recovered somewhat during the second world war while crop yields gradually increased (see Tables II.1, II.2, III.3 and II.5 for crop acreages and Tables IV.1, IV.2 and IV.3 for crop yields); the area under permanent grass apparently declined but some at least of the reduction can be attributed to changes in classification which resulted in a substantial rise in the area of 'mountain and heathland used for grazing'; livestock numbers fell in the Scottish Highlands but rose, even appreciably, in the upland counties of Wales and northern England which were nearer the main centres of population and were better placed to exploit the rising market for liquid milk, especially after the founding of the Milk Marketing Boards in the early 1930's (see Tables III.1, III.2, III.3 and III.5). Upland agriculture survived the depression because livestock prices (excepting wool) held up much better than cereal prices. Another advantage was the fall in the price of feedingstuffs which went some way towards easing the problem of winter feed. But at the same time the delicate equilibrium of the small farm economy was upset by the decline of local industry and reduction in the stock of by-employments. At one extreme, in the industrial parts of the West Riding, for instance, small farms were flourishing and prior to the First World War were producing as much as £40 an acre supplying the towns with milk, dairy produce, poultry and specialised crops like rhubarb. At the other, in the Scottish Highlands, vast tracts of land went out of agricultural use altogether as is evidenced by the vast expansion in the area under deer forest which rose from around 2 million acres in 1883 to over 3.5 million acres in 1912 (see Table II.11). It was this problem, the fundamentally low physical productivity of marginal hill land and its tendency to run to waste, that caught the attention of Stapledon in the 1930's and stimulated research into grassland improvement. But nowhere were the technical disabilities of upland farming ever properly overcome so that the most important factor determining the course of output and productivity, and the prime incentive, was that of price. The recovery in livestock numbers in the mid-1930's can be attributed to the modest improvement in prices following the imposition of import controls, and the continuing increase after 1940 to still higher prices and government subsidies (see also Figures 1, 2, 3, 4, 7, 8, 9 and 10).

## CONSTRAINTS ON UPLAND INDUSTRY AFTER 1880

The broader constraints on the growth of manufacturing industry in the upland zone have been touched upon and may be amplified by comparing the experience of three different industries — Hebridean tweed, Welsh woollens and Highland aluminium — which exhibited the extremes of response.

The textile industry in the Outer Hebrides enjoyed the greatest continuity among Highland industries although its survival and particular concentration is difficult to explain. One explanation, recently advanced, is that the Outer Hebrides were in need of a replacement economy to follow the kelp and fishing booms, that cottage tweed fitted well in an area with a high density of rural settlement and a strong attachment to the land, and that the industry was carefully promoted and organised. Equally, if not more important, was the nature of the product itself, its unique quality and export appeal, which rendered it less susceptible to competition than the cheaper, mass-produced fabrics. The Harris Tweed Association was founded in 1934 to promote and safeguard the product and to reconcile the competing interests of the hand-spun industry of Harris and the mill-spun industry of Lewis. The result was "a skilful balance . . . between a true domestic craft product, selling in limited quantities at a high price, and a mass produced article" (Moisley, 1961). The expansion of the industry after 1900 was achieved within a framework of modest technical change; the adoption, first, of small carding machines and foot-operated looms followed, in the 1930's, by factory mills and the mechanisation of the spinning, dyeing and finishing processes. The tweed industry was the economic salvation of Lewis where, in 1938, its value was put at £307 024 compared with £262 529 in fishing and £195 055 (or less than £50 a croft) in agriculture.

Whereas the Hebridean tweed industry survived and expanded between the wars, the Welsh woollen industry, despite its higher level of mechanisation, all but disappeared. In contrast to the Scottish industry, its traditional products — tweed and flannel — declined in popularity, and although distinctive, were at the same time cheap and utilitarian. The Welsh textile industry failed to adapt to changes in fashion and as knitted underwear replaced the traditional flannel, and the hard, thick tweed suitings produced by the factories went out of favour, so the industry declined. The combination of 'inferior goods', antiquated techniques and inefficient marketing proved fatal, and it is unlikely that Welsh entrepreneurs, even had they invested in new products, would have undercut the specialised hosiery manufacturers of the East Midlands. "Flannel is now only worn by babies and old people" said a contemporary in 1927. "The flannel trade of former times will never come back; it went out with flannel petticoats". (Jenkins, 1969). Indicatively, the hand-knitting factory established at Blaenau Ffestiniog in 1915 closed in 1918 when government contracts ceased, as did workshops at Bangor and Carnarvon, none of which could compete with electrically-powered machines.

Hydro-electricity promised for a time to revolutionise an economy heavily dependant on imported fuels. There was an interesting historical parallel for, in the same way as in the 18th century cheap wood fuel had attracted lowland iron-masters, so, after 1890, cheap electricity derived from highland water catchments was bait for the aluminium smelting industry. Smelting works were built at Foyers (1896), Kinlochleven (1909) and Fort William (1929-1943) in north-west Scotland, and at Conway Valley in North Wales (1907-1909). In 1910 the Scottish Highlands produced 20% of world aluminium, but the position was not held and neither did aluminium nor hydro-electricity ever become launching pads for industrialisation.

The British Aluminium Company's Kinlochleven project was a case in point and would seem to confirm that the multiplier effect of capital intensive industry in the raw materials sector was not uncommonly weak. Aluminium ore was imported; crude metal exported; plant, management and the majority of skilled labour were brought in from other regions; and profits were repatriated to London and not re-invested in the local economy. True, it provided work for a number of crofters, impoverished fisherfolk and unemployed quarrymen, but the work force, after the construction work had been completed, was very much less than the 6000 originally planned for. A limiting factor was the power supply itself. Even the Fort William works with its 85.7 MW generating station (cf 24.0 MW at Kinlochleven) was small by Canadian standards, and what was originally conceived as a major industry was contributing only 0.03% of total world production in 1970. In 1908 the British Aluminium Company (Gregor & Crichton, 1946) described the Kinlochleven project as, a "veritable 'back to the land' movement as full of hope and promise as any social reform at the time". Here, as at Foyers and Fort William, the company was responsible for its own infrastructure, but because of the shortfall in employment the company town was never large enough to support vital services, such as a hospital, a secondary school, a chemist, a laundry or even a cafe, which were located 16 miles away at Fort William. Critics of the scheme, of which there were many, claimed that the social advantages of a larger community were more than offset by its debilitating effect on the hinterland, which became entirely deserted.

## HYDRO-ELECTRICITY, WATER SUPPLY, FORESTRY AND RECREATION

Agriculture, mining and manufacturing did not generate a replacement economy and between 1880 and 1940 the volume of employment in all three sectors declined. Only the most compelling projects attracted investment while even local servicing industries were limited by the small size of the market and the ease with which everyday needs could be met by imports. In fact, the one comparative advantage enjoyed by the upland zone was its abundance of land and specialised topography and it was on these that the new forms of economic activity were based.

As early as 1890 hydro-electricity was used at some of the slate quarries in North Wales for lighting and for pumping water and, as already described, a number of aluminium smelting plants using hydro-electricity were established in north-west Scotland and North Wales between 1896 and 1933. Proximity to consumers was essential in the early days and it was only when power could be sold directly into the national grid that the construction of massive plants could be justified and the needs of local domestic consumers satisfied. Large-scale development in northern Scotland began only after the passing of the Hydro-Electric Development (Scotland) Act in 1943, and as late as 1948 only 7.3% of farms and 2.5% of crofts in the region were electrified. Elsewhere in Scotland, stations were built at the Falls of Clyde (1926), Rannoch (1930), Tummel (1933) and Galloway (1935-1936). In Snowdonia the North Wales Power and Traction Company was supplying current over 110 miles of power lines to local quarries in the early 1920's. But here, as elsewhere, it was soon discovered that only very few of the streams that had powered the forge- and textile-mills in the early Industrial Revolution were large enough to generate hydro-electricity. At the same time the development of larger catchments required expensive engineering works, and if, as was normally the case, the local demand was small, a large outside market was needed to take the surplus. In the early 1930's only 250.0 MW was generated, mostly in Scotland, and the electricity network was extended to the remoter part of Wales and the Scottish Highlands only after 1950, and at enormous cost.

As a result of the growth in population and concern about public health, the towns and cities of the industrial lowlands were already looking to the lakes and rivers of the hill regions as a potential source of freshwater in the 1840's. In the 1850's Glasgow began drawing water from Lake Katrine, 34 miles away; in the 1880's it built a reservoir at Craigmaddie and in 1919 purchased the whole of the lands comprising the watersheds of Lakes Arklet and Katrine to enlarge the catchment. In the Lake District, Manchester began to tap Thirlmere, near Helvellyn, in 1894, and before that in 1867, London itself was considering a conduit to Ullswater. The Manchester Corporation's Haweswater Dam, begun in 1929, was completed in 1941. Between 1880 and 1890 Liverpool Corporation dammed the Vrynog Valley to create the then largest single inland sheet of water in Wales and soon afterwards, in 1893-1904, Birmingham Corporation dammed the Elan Valley to form a reservoir supplying 75 million gallons a day. On the other side of the Pennines Bradford Corporation constructed two large reservoirs at the head of Nidderdale in 1904-1908 while, in South Wales, Swansea was forced to seek water at progressively higher levels after 1880 when the local supply was exhausted, culminating in the construction of the Upper Usk Reservoir (1955) whose catchment area rose to 1800 feet. By the early 1930's the upland zone supplied at least 65% of the national water supply, and 18 million people were supplied from the Pennines alone.

To many minds forestry was the most productive and potentially most profit-able land use in the more barren parts of the uplands. The Select Committee on Forestry Education (1887) acknowledged "the considerable social and economic advantages in an extensive system of planting in many parts of the Kingdom, especially in the West side of Ireland and in the Highlands of Scotland". It was argued in 1909 that the opportunity cost to agriculture of afforesting 8.5 million acres of unenclosed pasture lands in the Scottish Highlands and Welsh mountains was less than 5% of annual UK meat production. It is sometimes believed that afforestation in the upland zone was the unique achievement of the Forestry Commission, but in fact there was considerable planting by private landowners during the second half of the 19th century. In upland Scotland the forest area increased from 353 540 acres in 1845 to 707 453 acres in 1924 (see Table II.7). Most of the planting was in the more financially attractive areas, with the result that the greater part of the zone, especially where sport was a primary concern, and the more exposed coasts, was neglected. In Highland Scotland over 60% of all new planting between 1845 and 1914 was in Aberdeen, Nairn, Moray, Inverness and Perth.

The Forestry Commission was established in 1919 and though its initial impact was slight a start was made in redressing the balance within and between regions. For private foresters the limiting factors after 1920 were low prices and the extreme marginality of the land which tended to be poor in quality or at too high an altitude. Forestry, they argued, must be regarded as a national duty. Between 1924 and 1947-49, the forest area of upland Wales rose from 4.6 to 6.2% of the total land area and that of upland Scotland from 5.6 to 7.1%, a net gain of about a quarter of a million acres, most of it on Commission land (see Tables II.7, II.8, II.9 and II.10). The impact on employment is difficult to gauge because of differing requirements at successive stages of the forest cycle. Fewer workers were needed for maintenance than for planting and because of the immaturity of Commission forest little labour was employed in felling between 1920 and 1950. Employment opportunities between the wars would have been greater but for the massive fellings of mature and semi-mature trees on private estates during the First World War. Even so, numbers of forest workers in North Wales more than trebled between 1901 and 1951, and in Merioneth where the Commission had planted over 14 600 acres, they rose from 39 to 372. (See Figures 5 and 6.) A unique feature of Commission policy was the establishment of 'forest worker smallholdings' of which more than 1000 had been established by 1939.

Sport and tourism were also important and already by the late-19th century they were a mainstay of the local economy in parts of the Lake District and the Scottish Highlands. Sport was especially vital in Scotland. Interest in the great medieval sport of deer hunting revived in the early-19th century but only after 1850, when the railways opened up the region to the more casual sportsman, did landowners begin to realise the letting potential of a well-stocked moor. "Nothing is more fashionable than Highland sports", wrote Lauvegne in 1855. ". . . That bustle which, for two or three months in the year, awakens in the slumbering echoes of the rocks something like the gathering of the clans, results in handsome incomes to the proprietors". Numbers of Highland deer forests increased from 45 in 1838 to a peak of 203 in 1912 when they covered 3 584 916 acres. The conversion of sheep walk to deer forest grew apace following the fall in wool prices in the 1870's. Ambitious proprietors, who spent heavily on lodges and outdoor staff, reaped the benefit of high rents which, on the best estates, rose from £300 a year in 1833 to £5000 a year in 1905. In 1914 deer forests contributed nearly half the total rateable value of the county of Inverness and over one fifth that of Ross and Cromarty. The crofting community derived substantial benefit from the lease of sporting rights in the neighbourhood, and the presence of shooting tenants and their households was a valuable, albeit seasonal, source of income both to them and to the Highland Railway Company which profited from the conveyance of household supplies, and shooting and fishing parties. Between the wars deer-stalking declined in popularity in favour of grouse-shooting (which provided sport for more guns) and fishing. Winter sports were still in the embryonic stage; the Scottish Ski Club was founded in 1907 but attempts to establish permanent runs were frustrated by a succession of mild winters. Parts of the Scottish Highlands were used for snow and mountain warfare training in the Second World War and the beginning of the modern ski industry dates from the late 1940's when, following the hard winter of 1947 which brought a large number of civilians onto the slopes, land was made available to the Cairngorm Winter Sports Development Board in Glen More Forest Park.

The uplands were first discovered by tourists in the 18th century when 'taking the waters' became a fashionable pastime of the well-to-do, and a number of spas were established. Yet, except for Harrogate and Buxton, none became large 'medical' centres and most owed their popularity to other factors — the development of sporting facilities such as golf, fishing and shooting, or other tourist attractions in the neighbourhood. The greatest and most enduring asset, and main source of appeal, were the mountains and lakes themselves. "The taste for mountain scenery" said Trevelyan (1949), "grew *parri passu* with the Industrial Revolution". Formerly, the connoisseurs of scenery had preferred their landscapes tamed and planned and it was the Romantics in the late-18th century who taught people to look at nature with a new kind of pleasure and to revere wild and primitive places. Interest was at first confined to 'natural curiosities' but after 1820 travellers came more in search of the picturesque. Walking and rambling became popular after 1850. In the Lake District the age of mass-tourism began in 1847 with the railways which led to excursions of day-trippers from the industrial towns. In the 1860's, in the Yorkshire Dales, a landowner at Pately Bridge opened his woods and fishponds to the public at sixpence a visit, complete with guide book. Wensleydale was discovered following a railway extension in 1877 and, after 1885, brass band concerts were held at the waterfall at Hardraw Scar for the popular entertainment. Enthusiasm for the Scottish Highlands grew more slowly on account of their remoteness but Highland holidays became *beau monde* after Queen Victoria pioneered the 'Royal Route' to Inverness via the Great Glen. A new trend began in the 1880's when the country cottage, often an abandoned farmhouse or miner's dwelling, became a vogue, especially in Wales and the Pennines. All forms of tourism expanded between the wars with the advent of the motor car and charabanc which could penetrate areas hitherto inaccessible to the rail traveller. It was estimated that in 1924 some 60 000 people made the ascent of Snowdon which two centuries earlier Defoe had described as a hill of "monstrous height", the last refuge of the Ancient Britons.

The impact of tourism on the upland economy is difficult to measure. A number of towns, it is true, became important tourist centres but the benefits otherwise were thinly spread and in most parts would only slightly have affected income and employment. Compared with the seaside resorts, numbers of visitors were small and the season short while only a few towns such as Harrogate, Buxton and Llandrindod Wells had large resident populations. In 1953 only 8% of British holiday-makers visited Wales and most went to the northern coastal resorts. Upland Wales, however, and the Scottish Highlands, were more popular with foreign tourists. In 1954 a croft house in the Scottish Highlands might be let for £30 a month and more could be obtained where the owners had installed a bathroom and indoor sanitation. But the typical visitor did not require the same elaborate services and entertainments as the seaside holidaymaker. Nor did upland agriculture supply even his food, most of which was imported. It was remarked in 1954 that in parts of the Scottish Highlands where there were hedges of fuchsia and where palm and eucalyptus grew in the open, it was all but impossible to obtain locally-grown fresh fruit and vegetables in the month of August, with bread bought from Glasgow and fish from Aberdeen.

## THE UPLAND ECONOMY AND THE NATION

In conclusion, it would seem that the greatest opportunity for sustained economic growth in the upland zone occurred during the early Industrial Revolution before the age of coal and iron and the establishment of a free trade economy. That chance was lost and thereafter the balance of comparative advantage between regions perceptibly shifted and the income and productivity gap between the uplands and lowlands progressively widened. Trade and investment flows assumed a pattern similar to that between rich and poor nations and primary and secondary producers in the world economy. Since the 1930's the nature of that relationship has changed only inasmuch as the local structure has been reinforced by institutional elements imposed by central government, in the form of increased public expenditure, the development of the social infrastructure, and the establishment of a system of fiscal and financial incentives. In the 1930's more than ten shillings a week on average was paid to families in the crofting districts under the national insurance and assistance schemes. In 1950 income per head of population in the region was less than 75% of the UK level and of that a higher than average proportion consisted of welfare payments and subsidies. The occupational census is instructive because it shows that most of the new employment created in Merionethshire between 1901 and 1951 was in the public sector, in transport, utilities, administration, state forestry and defence (see Table I.10).

In view of the small economic value of the hill lands it may seem a little strange that there was so much conflict as to their use. Conflict was already apparent in the crofting districts of Scotland before 1800 and by the late-19th century the uplands generally had become a bone of contention between farmers, foresters, sportsmen, landowners, industrialists, conservationists and tourists. It is ironical, but also indicative, that the poet Wordsworth who had done so much to popularise the Lake District among his own kind should have been bitterly opposed to mass-tourism. He upbraided the railway companies for laying on excursion trains and "tempting the humbler classes to leave their homes" (Bouch & Jones, 1961), and for much the same reason, took to task a local farmer for using a mowing machine instead of the traditional scythe in the hayfield.

Economic decline and depopulation were of little moment to interest groups for whom the appeal of the upland zone was its deserted landscapes. The real issues were blurred and not often debated but were nicely put in 1802 by the road engineer, Thomas Telford, in his evidence to a government committee enquiring into the effects of the Highland Clearances (British Parliamentary Papers, 1802-1803):

"In one points of view it may be stated, that, taking the mountainous Parts of Scotland as a District of the British Empire, it is the Interest of the Empire that this District be made to produce as much human Food as it is capable of doing at the least possible Expense; that this may be done by stocking it chiefly with Sheep; that it is the interest of the Empire the food so produced should not be consumed by Persons residing amongst the Mountains totally unemployed, but rather in some other Parts of the Country, where their Labour can be made productive either in the business of Agriculture, Fisheries or Manufactures . . .

In another point of View it may be stated, that it is a great Hardship, if not a great Injustice, that the Inhabitants of an extensive District should all at once be driven from their native Country, to make way for Sheep Farming; . . . that, in a few Years, this Excess will be evidence; that before it is discovered, the Country will be depopulated, and that Race of People which has of late years maintained to honourable a Share in the Operations of our Armies and Natives will then be no more . . ."

The problem then, as now, was to define the local as against the national interest, to reconcile them, and to decide, as a matter of policy, whether to reverse the historical trend of upland migration, or whether to allow the level of economic activity and of population to be determined by market forces. Except in the crofting districts, which were a special case, the official attitude before the 1930's was one of laissez-faire. Government intervention since the Second World War has confirmed the view that if economics is the dismal science then regional economics was its most advanced branch. Historical experience underlines the weight of the problem, and the emptiness of the upland landscape — the abandoned mines, derelict factories and deserted farmhouses — testifies to the unevenness of the struggle. The challenge facing the upland economist today may be likened to that of geographers in the early-18th century who, said Defoe (1962 edition), were at such a loss to describe the north of Scotland that, "they are oblig'd to fill it up with hills and mountains, as they do the inner parts of Africa, with lyons and elephants, for want of knowing what else to put there".

The deer forest at Glenesk, Angus. In many parts of the Scottish Highlands deerstalking replaced sheep-farming as the main animal enterprise in the late-19th century. In 1911, there were 3.5 million acres of deer forest in Scotland, and shooting — the most extensive form of land use — was sometimes the most profitable part of the local economy.

'Umbrella' farming at Ysgubor, Dinas Mawddwy, Merioneth, 1966. The main agricultural enterprise of the Highland zone is sheep rearing and the main problem, now and historically, was the shortage of winter feed. Many hearts were broken and fortunes lost in trying to introduce more intensive systems of farming based on fodder crops. This photograph of a trial demonstration of kale and swede for ewe lambs illustrates the mood of the hills and the enormity of the problem.

Winter ploughing, Vale of Grasmere, Lake District, 1949. Many upland grazings were ploughed up in the Second World War after 70 or more years under permanent grass.

Croft and thatched poultry houses at Eriskay, Inverness, c. 1950. The poultry houses were the original croft. The new croft, with corrugated-iron roof, was built probably between the wars using cheap building materials provided by the Government. Electricity was laid on after the Second World War.

Mountain shed in Montgomery, c. 1950. The shed or, as in Scotland, the 'shieling' was essential to sheep-farming on the higher upland pastures.

A paring spade in use in the Brechfa area, Carmarthen, 1890. The paring spade was commonly used in the hill areas of south-west England, Wales and the Pennines for breaking-up old grassland and converting hill slopes to arable. Often, the turves were burnt and the ash used as fertiliser.

Ploughing by oxen with a traditional type of Orkney plough, c. 1900.

The Sutherland Reclamations, 1872-1878. This was the most spectacular attempt to reclaim the moorlands for mixed farming. Altogether, 2643 acres were improved, using steam ploughs, at a cost of £254 000. Most of this arable land reverted to grass after 1880.

Drying hay by the rack method in Ross-shire. The hay harvest in the Highlands and Islands was, and still is, a difficult operation in wet summers.

Transporting hay by sledge cart in Brithdir, Merioneth, c. 1910. Wheeled carts were rare in upland Wales on account of the uneven terrain and bad roads.

41

Flailing oats in Orkney, c. 1885. In the background is a traditional Orkney house.

Mr & Mrs Jones, of Ffynnonoer, near Cardigan, spreading dung for potatoes. The potato became a staple item of diet in many upland areas after 1750.

43

A flock of sheep near the source of the Wye, Montgomery, 1949, on recently improved hill pasture.

Shearing sheep near Cader Idris, Merioneth, c. 1910. The shearing was sometimes done by migrant workers but more often by 'neighbours' working local farms in rotation.

Lamb sale at Forest Farm, Invershin, Bonar Bridge, Sutherland, c. 1940. Sheep replaced black cattle as the chief grazing animal in the Scottish highlands between 1750 and 1820.

Fair Day at St. Clears, Carmarthen. The heyday of the small market town was in the mid-19th century whence they declined as marketing and local manufacturing centres.

47

A water-powered saw-mill, Glenesk, Angus, c. 1900.

Floating logs on the Upper Spey, Scotland, c. 1890. One of the main problems of timber production in the Highlands was that of extraction and the River Spey was an important outlet for log-timber from the fir forests of Strath Spey and Rothiemurchus.

A saw-mill at Potarch in Ballogie Forest, Aberdeen, where in the early 1950's, a new village, Jonesville, was built to house Forestry Commission workers. The devastation in the background is the result of the great gale of February 1953.

The Dorothea Slate Quarry, North Wales, c. 1890. North Wales was the main centre of slate production in Britain. In 1890, Merioneth produced 95% of Britain's mined slate and Caernarvon 92% of Britain's quarried slate.

51

Dylife Lead Mine, Montgomery, c. 1900. Lead and zinc were widely distributed throughout upland Wales and mining reached a peak in the late-1870's. Thereafter it declined because of foreign competition and the exhaustion of deposits.

Van Lead Mine, near Llanidloes, Montogmery, c. 1890. Most lead mines were tiny, but the Van was one of the largest and most profitable, raising 96 000 tons of lead ore, 28 000 tons of zinc ore and 800 000 ounces of silver during its working life.

Vivian Slate Quarry, Llanberis, Caernarvon, 1896. This was one of the largest Welsh slate quarries which installed advanced mechanical techniques such as the conveyor-system here depicted.

Dressing slates at a quarry in Appin, Argyll, c. 1930. The Highlands had many slate deposits but these were not developed intensively because of the high cost of transport and Welsh competition.

Locomotive 'Velinheli' Dinorwic Slate Quarry, Caernarvon, c. 1910. Larger mining companies had to invest heavily in rail and tramways in remote mountain areas. The Dinorwic tramroad, built in 1816, was carrying over 100 000 tons a year in the 1860's. The Padarn

Panning for gold in North Wales, c. 1890. Gold was discovered in North Wales at Cwm Einon in 1843. Since the 1850's, Merioneth has yielded 150 000 ounces of gold. Even at its peak the Welsh gold industry only employed less than 250 men. It collapsed in the 1920's when the lodes ran dry but a last burst of activity at Beddcoeddwr Mine produced enough gold for Princess Marina's wedding ring. Gold was also discovered in Sutherland in the late-1860's.

Scrabster Harbour, Caithness, c. 1890. Fish-gutting and fish-packing were an important source of employment for women in the High-lands and Islands, some of whom migrated hundreds of miles for that purpose following the herring up and down the coast. The herring fishery grew rapidly after 1820 and was flourishing in the 1890's. It declined after 1920 as a result of the loss of export markets in

Sharing out the catch, Birsay, Orkney, c. 1935. Fishing was done by small farmers from open boats.

Cutting sea-weed in the Aran Islands, Galway, Ireland, Sea-weed is still used by local farmers as a fertiliser.

Burning kelp in Orkney, c. 1900. The manufacture of kelp or sea-weed ash was an important industry on the Scottish West Coast and Islands between 1730 and 1840. It was a main source of soda, potash and iodine and survived in Orkney until the First World War.

Cutting peat at Abergwesyn, Brecon, 1938. Peat was the main fuel in many upland areas and peat-cutting was a normal part of the seasonal round.

A decayed rural industry: wheel-lathe turning in Cardigan. Few of the traditional craft industries survived the First World War.

Clog-making in Ty'ny'wern and Tre'r-ddol, Cardigan, c. 1910. Clog-making was locally important up to the First World War. Roving bands of clog-sole cutters used to visit Central Wales to fell alder wood and make clog-sole blocks for sale in Lancashire and South Wales.

Interior of a Welsh weaving mill. These mills, using cheap water power and local wool, multiplied in upland Wales during the first half of the 19th century. After a promising start, the Welsh textile industry flagged after 1880.

Wool spinning, Middle Mill, Solva, Pembroke, c. 1928. The adoption of spinning machinery did not oust the spinning wheel which was still common in cottage households in the late-19th century.

Textile manufacture, Alltcafen Mills in Caernarvon. Most Welsh mills were small, but a few larger mills, driven by steam and water power, were erected in the third quarter of the 19th century.

Stall at Carmarthen market selling local Welsh cloth, c. 1936. Demand for the hard, thick tweed-suitings was then declining and manufacturers were unable to switch to more fashionable fabrics.

# Appendices I–V

Appendix I:  The population of upland Britain, 1801-1951

Table I.1
THE POPULATION OF ENGLAND, 1801-1951 (Thousands)

| | 1801 | 1821 | 1841 | 1861 | 1881 | 1901 | 1911 | 1921 | 1931 | 1951 |
|---|---|---|---|---|---|---|---|---|---|---|
| ENGLAND | | | | | | | | | | |
| Westmorland | 41 | 51 | 56 | 61 | 64 | 64 | 64 | 66 | 65 | 67 |
| Cumberland | 117 | 156 | 178 | 205 | 251 | 267 | 266 | 273 | 263 | 285 |
| TOTAL 1 | 158 | 207 | 234 | 266 | 315 | 331 | 330 | 339 | 328 | 352 |
| Derbyshire | 162 | 214 | 272 | 339 | 462 | 596 | 679 | 709 | 750 | 826 |
| Durham | 149 | 194 | 308 | 509 | 867 | 1 187 | 1 370 | 1 479 | 1 486 | 1 464 |
| Northumberland | 168 | 213 | 266 | 343 | 434 | 603 | 697 | 746 | 757 | 798 |
| Yorkshire — North Riding | 158 | 187 | 203 | 242 | 341 | 377 | 419 | 456 | 467 | 525 |
| Yorkshire — West Riding | 591 | 833 | 1 195 | 1 553 | 2 237 | 2 843 | 3 131 | 3 270 | 3 446 | 3 586 |
| TOTAL 2 | 1 228 | 1 641 | 2 244 | 2 986 | 4 341 | 5 606 | 6 296 | 6 660 | 6 906 | 7 199 |
| UPLAND ENGLAND TOTAL (1 + 2) | 1 386 | 1 848 | 2 478 | 3 252 | 4 656 | 5 937 | 6 626 | 6 999 | 7 234 | 7 551 |
| ALL ENGLAND TOTAL | 8 352 | 11 282 | 15 003 | 18 945 | 24 613 | 30 813 | 34 043 | 35 679 | 37 791 | 41 584 |

Source:  Mitchell (1962).

Note:  The above counties will be referred to as 'upland England' in the following tables.

**Table I.2**
THE POPULATION OF WALES, 1801-1951 (Thousands)

| | 1801 | 1821 | 1841 | 1861 | 1881 | 1901 | 1911 | 1921 | 1931 | 1951 |
|---|---|---|---|---|---|---|---|---|---|---|
| **WALES** | | | | | | | | | | |
| Brecon | 32 | 44 | 56 | 62 | 58 | 54 | 59 | 61 | 58 | 57 |
| Caernarvon | 42 | 58 | 81 | 96 | 119 | 123 | 123 | 128 | 121 | 124 |
| Cardigan | 43 | 58 | 69 | 72 | 70 | 61 | 60 | 61 | 55 | 53 |
| Carmarthen | 67 | 90 | 106 | 112 | 125 | 135 | 160 | 175 | 179 | 172 |
| Merioneth | 30 | 34 | 39 | 47 | 52 | 49 | 46 | 45 | 43 | 41 |
| Montgomery | 48 | 60 | 70 | 67 | 66 | 55 | 53 | 51 | 48 | 46 |
| Radnor | 19 | 23 | 25 | 25 | 24 | 23 | 23 | 24 | 21 | 20 |
| TOTAL 1 | 281 | 367 | 446 | 481 | 514 | 500 | 524 | 545 | 525 | 513 |
| Flint | 39 | 54 | 67 | 70 | 81 | 81 | 93 | 107 | 113 | 145 |
| Denbigh | 60 | 76 | 88 | 101 | 112 | 134 | 147 | 158 | 158 | 171 |
| TOTAL 2 | 99 | 130 | 155 | 171 | 193 | 215 | 240 | 265 | 271 | 316 |
| UPLAND WALES TOTAL (1 + 2) | 380 | 497 | 601 | 652 | 707 | 715 | 764 | 810 | 796 | 829 |
| ALL WALES TOTAL | 541 | 718 | 911 | 1121 | 1361 | 1715 | 2027 | 2208 | 2161 | 2174 |

Note: The above counties will be referred to as 'upland Wales' in the following tables.

Source: Mitchell (1962)

**Table I.3**
THE POPULATION OF SCOTLAND, 1801-1951 (Thousands)

| | 1801 | 1821 | 1841 | 1861 | 1881 | 1901 | 1911 | 1921 | 1931 | 1951 |
|---|---|---|---|---|---|---|---|---|---|---|
| **SCOTLAND** | | | | | | | | | | |
| Aberdeen (−Aberdeen City) | 94 | 111 | 129 | 148 | 162 | 150 | 148 | 142 | 130 | 125 |
| Argyllshire | 81 | 97 | 97 | 80 | 76 | 74 | 71 | 77 | 63 | 63 |
| Banffshire | 37 | 44 | 50 | 59 | 63 | 60 | 61 | 57 | 55 | 50 |
| Caithness | 23 | 29 | 36 | 41 | 39 | 34 | 32 | 28 | 26 | 23 |
| Invernesshire | 73 | 90 | 98 | 89 | 90 | 90 | 87 | 82 | 82 | 85 |
| Moray | 28 | 31 | 35 | 43 | 44 | 45 | 43 | 42 | 41 | 48 |
| Nairn | 8 | 9 | 9 | 10 | 10 | 9 | 9 | 9 | 8 | 9 |
| Orkney | 24 | 27 | 31 | 32 | 32 | 29 | 26 | 24 | 22 | 21 |
| Perthshire | 126 | 138 | 137 | 134 | 129 | 123 | 124 | 126 | 121 | 128 |
| Ross and Cromarty | 56 | 69 | 79 | 81 | 78 | 76 | 77 | 71 | 63 | 61 |
| Shetland | 22 | 26 | 31 | 32 | 30 | 28 | 28 | 26 | 21 | 19 |
| Sutherland | 23 | 24 | 25 | 25 | 23 | 21 | 20 | 18 | 16 | 14 |
| | | | | | | | | | | |
| UPLAND SCOTLAND TOTAL | 595 | 695 | 757 | 774 | 776 | 739 | 726 | 702 | 648 | 646 |
| City of Aberdeen | 27 | 44 | 63 | 74 | 106 | 154 | 164 | 159 | 170 | 183 |
| | | | | | | | | | | |
| ALL SCOTLAND TOTAL | 1608 | 2092 | 2620 | 3062 | 3736 | 4472 | 4761 | 4882 | 4843 | 5096 |

Note: The above counties will be referred to as 'upland Scotland' in the following tables.

Source: Mitchell (1962)

**Table I.4**
THE POPULATION OF NORTHERN IRELAND, 1801-1951 (Thousands)

| | 1801 | 1821 | 1841 | 1861 | 1881 | 1901 | 1911 | 1926 | 1937 | 1951 |
|---|---|---|---|---|---|---|---|---|---|---|
| **NORTHERN IRELAND** | | | | | | | | | | |
| Antrim | — | 234 | 291 | 257 | 238 | 196 | 194 | 192 | 197 | 231 |
| Armagh | — | 197 | 233 | 190 | 163 | 125 | 120 | 110 | 109 | 114 |
| Down | — | 325 | 361 | 299 | 248 | 206 | 204 | 209 | 211 | 241 |
| Fermanagh | — | 131 | 157 | 106 | 85 | 65 | 62 | 58 | 55 | 53 |
| Londonderry | — | 194 | 222 | 184 | 165 | 144 | 141 | 140 | 143 | 156 |
| Tyrone | — | 262 | 313 | 239 | 198 | 151 | 143 | 133 | 128 | 132 |
| **UPLAND NORTHERN IRELAND TOTAL** | 1030 (Estimated) | 1343 | 1577 | 1275 | 1097 | 887 | 864 | 842 | 843 | 927 |
| City of Belfast | 20 (Estimated) | 37 | 70 | 122 | 208 | 349 | 387 | 415 | 438 | 444 |
| **ALL NORTHERN IRELAND TOTAL** | 1050 | 1380 | 1647 | 1397 | 1305 | 1236 | 1251 | 1257 | 1281 | 1371 |

Source: Mitchell (1962)

**Table I.5**
THE POPULATION OF THE UNITED KINGDOM, 1801-1951 (Thousands)

| | 1801 | 1821 | 1841 | 1861 | 1881 | 1901 | 1911 | 1921 | 1931 | 1951 |
|---|---|---|---|---|---|---|---|---|---|---|
| Upland England | 1 386 | 1 848 | 2 478 | 3 252 | 4 656 | 5 937 | 6 626 | 6 999 | 7 234 | 7 551 |
| ALL ENGLAND | 8 352 | 11 282 | 15 003 | 18 945 | 24 613 | 30 813 | 34 043 | 35 679 | 37 791 | 41 584 |
| Upland Wales | 380 | 497 | 601 | 652 | 707 | 715 | 764 | 810 | 796 | 829 |
| ALL WALES | 541 | 718 | 911 | 1 121 | 1 361 | 1 715 | 2 027 | 2 208 | 2 161 | 2 174 |
| Upland Scotland | 595 | 695 | 757 | 774 | 776 | 739 | 726 | 702 | 648 | 646 |
| ALL SCOTLAND | 1 608 | 2 092 | 2 620 | 3 062 | 3 736 | 4 472 | 4 761 | 4 882 | 4 843 | 5 096 |
| Upland Northern Ireland | 1 030 | 1 343 | 1 577 | 1 275 | 1 097 | 887 | 864 | 842 | 843 | 927 |
| ALL NORTHERN IRELAND | 1 050 | 1 380 | 1 647 | 1 397 | 1 305 | 1 236 | 1 251 | 1 257 | 1 281 | 1 371 |
| Upland United Kingdom | 3 391 | 4 383 | 5 413 | 5 953 | 7 236 | 8 278 | 8 980 | 9 353 | 9 521 | 9 953 |
| ALL UNITED KINGDOM | 11 551 | 15 472 | 20 181 | 24 525 | 31 015 | 38 236 | 42 082 | 44 026 | 46 076 | 50 225 |

Sources: Tables I.1, I.2, I.3 & I.4

Table I.6
## THE PROPORTION OF EACH COUNTRY'S POPULATION IN UPLAND AREAS, 1801-1951 (per cent)

|  | 1801 | 1821 | 1841 | 1861 | 1881 | 1901 | 1911 | 1921 | 1931 | 1951 |
|---|---|---|---|---|---|---|---|---|---|---|
| ENGLAND | 16.6 | 16.4 | 16.5 | 17.2 | 18.9 | 19.3 | 19.5 | 19.6 | 19.1 | 18.2 |
| WALES | 70.2 | 69.2 | 66.0 | 58.2 | 51.9 | 41.7 | 37.7 | 36.7 | 36.8 | 38.1 |
| SCOTLAND | 37.0 | 33.2 | 28.9 | 25.3 | 20.8 | 16.5 | 15.2 | 14.4 | 13.4 | 12.7 |
| NORTHERN IRELAND | 98.1 | 97.3 | 95.7 | 91.3 | 84.1 | 71.8 | 69.1 | 67.0 | 65.8 | 67.6 |
| UNITED KINGDOM | 29.4 | 28.3 | 26.8 | 24.3 | 23.3 | 21.6 | 21.3 | 21.2 | 20.7 | 19.8 |

Source: Table I.5

Table I.7
## RATES OF CHANGE OF POPULATION IN THE UNITED KINGDOM, 1801-1951 (per cent)

|  | 1851/1801 | 1901/1851 | 1951/1901 |
|---|---|---|---|
| Westmorland/Cumberland | 60.1 | 30.8 | 6.3 |
| Rest of upland England | 109.3 | 118.1 | 28.4 |
| All upland England | 103.7 | 110.3 | 27.2 |
| ALL ENGLAND | 102.6 | 82.1 | 35.0 |
| Flint/Denbigh | 62.6 | 33.5 | 47.0 |
| Rest of upland Wales | 64.4 | 8.2 | 2.6 |
| All upland Wales | 86.0 | 14.8 | 15.9 |
| ALL WALES | 86.9 | 70.5 | 26.8 |
| Upland Scotland | 30.8 | (−)5.0 | (−)12.6 |
| ALL SCOTLAND | 79.7 | 54.8 | 14.0 |
| Upland Northern Ireland | 31.6 | (−)34.5 | 4.5 |
| ALL NORTHERN IRELAND | 38.9 | (−)15.2 | 10.9 |
| Upland United Kingdom | 64.5 | 48.4 | 20.2 |
| ALL UNITED KINGDOM | 92.8 | 71.7 | 31.4 |

Sources: Tables I.1, I.2, I.3 & I.4; Mitchell (1962).

## Table I.8
THE PROPORTION OF THE POPULATION EMPLOYED IN AGRICULTURE COMPARED WITH THE OCCUPIED POPULATION IN SCOTLAND, 1871, 1911 and 1931 (per cent)

|      | In Scotland | In the Highlands |
|------|-------------|------------------|
| 1871 | 16.5        | 40.5             |
| 1911 | 7.5         | 23.6             |
| 1931 | 7.3         | 22.6             |

Source: Extracted from Bryden & Houston (1976). See note below.

## Table I.9
THE OCCUPIED POPULATION IN SCOTLAND AND THE HIGHLANDS AND ISLANDS, 1871, 1911 and 1931 (per cent)

|      | Total occupied population in the Highlands as a proportion of Scotland | Population occupied in agriculture: the Highlands as a proportion of Scotland |
|------|------------------------------------------------------------------------|------------------------------------------------------------------------------|
| 1871 | 9.7  | 23.9 |
| 1911 | 7.3  | 23.1 |
| 1931 | 5.7  | 17.5 |

Source: Extracted from Bryden & Houston (1976). See note below.

Note: In an appendix relating to the above two tables, Bryden & Houston (1976) discuss the problems involved in comparing census data over time. They stress in this case that variations in the census definitions of agricultural employment and employment in general made analysis difficult, and comparisons should be made with care.

The Highlands were consistently defined as the 7 crofting counties (Shetland, Orkney, Sutherland, Caithness, Ross and Cromarty, Inverness and Argyll). For each census date, sub-divisions which did not refer directly to agricultural employment were omitted.

Table I.10

DISTRIBUTION OF THE MALE LABOUR FORCE IN MAIN OCCUPATIONS
IN MERIONETHSHIRE, 1851, 1901 and 1951 (per cent)

|  | 1851 | 1901 | 1951 |
|---|---|---|---|
| Agriculture, horticulture, forestry and fishing | 52.0 | 29.3 | 21.2 |
| Mining and quarrying | 9.9 | 28.6[1] | 9.0 |
| Chemicals | — | — | 2.2 |
| Engineering, vehicles and metal goods | 3.6 | 2.3 | 2.3 |
| Textiles | 3.3 | 1.7 | 0.2 |
| Clothing and footwear | 2.8 | 2.8 | 0.4 |
| Leather and leather goods | 0.7 | 0.5 | — |
| Food, drink and tobacco | 1.1 | 0.8 | 1.5 |
| Wood and cork | 1.0 | 0.5 | 0.6 |
| Paper and printing | 0.2 | 0.6 | 0.4 |
| Building and construction | 4.6 | 7.3 | 8.0 |
| Transport, communications and public utilities | 3.7 | 7.6 | 7.8 |
| Distributive trades | 3.1 | 5.1 | 6.6 |
| Public administration and defence | 0.3 | 1.6 | 26.9 |
| Professional and other services | 3.9 | 8.2 | 9.5 |
| Labourers (branch undefined) | 6.0 | 2.5 | 0.1 |

1   Predominantly slate quarrying.

Source: GB Census.

# Appendix II: The land use of upland Britain, 1790-1950

## Table II.1
### THE LAND USE OF UPLAND BRITAIN, 1889 (Acres)

| | Arable land | Permanent grass | Total area under crops and grass | Mountain and heathland used for grazing[1] |
|---|---|---|---|---|
| Upland England | 1 618 229 | 2 973 288 | 4 591 517 | 1 382 519 |
| ALL ENGLAND | 12 290 441 | 12 700 574 | 24 991 015 | 1 861 829 |
| Upland Wales | 668 927 | 1 444 434 | 2 113 361 | 818 122 |
| ALL WALES | 904 500 | 1 949 417 | 2 853 917 | 953 234 |
| Upland Scotland | 1 608 912 | 386 190 | 1 995 102 | 6 789 026 |
| ALL SCOTLAND | 3 672 553 | 1 215 872 | 4 888 425 | 9 272 169 |
| Upland Great Britain | 3 896 068 | 4 803 912 | 8 699 980 | 8 989 667 |
| ALL GREAT BRITAIN | 16 867 494 | 15 865 863 | 32 733 357 | 12 087 232 |

1   1892 figures used as none available for 1889.

Sources:   Board of Agriculture (1889 & 1892)

## Table II.2
### THE LAND USE OF UPLAND BRITAIN, 1919 (Acres)

| | Arable land | Permanent grass | Total area under crops and grass | Mountain and heathland used for grazing |
|---|---|---|---|---|
| Upland England | 1 529 549 | 2 859 259 | 4 388 808 | 1 740 368 |
| ALL ENGLAND | 11 412 347 | 12 656 945 | 24 069 292 | 2 722 837 |
| Upland Wales | 643 196 | 1 347 681 | 1 990 877 | 1 215 425 |
| ALL WALES | 896 529 | 1 782 132 | 2 678 661 | 1 398 617 |
| Upland Scotland | 1 575 342 | 356 456 | 1 931 798 | 6 743 035 |
| ALL SCOTLAND | 3 408 479 | 1 342 996 | 4 751 475 | 9 488 542 |
| Upland Great Britain | 3 748 087 | 4 563 396 | 8 311 483 | 9 698 828 |
| ALL GREAT BRITAIN | 15 717 355 | 15 782 073 | 31 499 428 | 13 609 996 |

Sources: Board of Agriculture for Scotland (1920); Ministry of Agriculture and Fisheries (1920).

**Table II.3**
THE LAND USE OF UPLAND BRITAIN, 1949 (Acres)

| | Arable land | Permanent grass | Total area under crops and grass | Mountain and heathland used for grazing |
|---|---|---|---|---|
| Upland England | 1 798 111 | 2 005 237 | 3 803 348 | 2 177 829 |
| ALL ENGLAND | 12 860 529 | 8 972 481 | 21 833 010 | 3 669 549 |
| Upland Wales | 721 061 | 1 005 623 | 1 726 644 | 1 525 162 |
| ALL WALES | 1 063 137 | 1 483 983 | 2 547 120 | 1 855 949 |
| Upland Scotland | 1 485 648 | 331 938 | 1 817 586 | 7 987 272 |
| ALL SCOTLAND | 3 228 069 | 1 188 232 | 4 416 301 | 10 948 971 |
| Upland Great Britain | 4 004 820 | 3 342 798 | 7 347 578 | 11 690 263 |
| ALL GREAT BRITAIN | 17 151 735 | 11 644 696 | 28 796 431 | 16 474 469 |

Sources: Department of Agriculture for Scotland (1952); Ministry of Agriculture and Fisheries (1952).

Table II.4
THE LAND USE OF UPLAND BRITAIN, 1889, 1919 and 1949 (Acres)

| | 1889 | | 1919 | | 1949 | |
|---|---|---|---|---|---|---|
| | Upland Great Britain | ALL GREAT BRITAIN | Upland Great Britain | ALL GREAT BRITAIN | Upland Great Britain | ALL GREAT BRITAIN |
| Arable land | 3 896 068 | 16 867 494 | 3 748 087 | 15 717 355 | 4 004 820 | 17 151 735 |
| Permanent grass | 4 803 912 | 15 865 863 | 4 563 396 | 15 782 073 | 3 342 798 | 11 644 696 |
| Total area under crops and grass | 8 699 980 | 32 733 357 | 8 311 483 | 31 499 428 | 7 347 578 | 28 796 431 |
| Mountain and heathland used for grazing | 8 989 667 | 12 087 232 | 9 698 828 | 13 609 996 | 11 690 263 | 16 474 469 |

Sources: Tables II.1, II.2 & II.3.

# Table II.5

THE PROPORTION OF EACH TYPE OF LAND USE TO THE TOTAL LAND AREA OF UPLAND BRITAIN, 1889, 1919 and 1949 (per cent)

| | 1889 | | 1919 | | 1949 | |
|---|---|---|---|---|---|---|
| | Upland Great Britain | ALL GREAT BRITAIN | Upland Great Britain | ALL GREAT BRITAIN | Upland Great Britain | ALL GREAT BRITAIN |
| Arable land | 16.6 | 30.0 | 16.0 | 28.0 | 17.1 | 30.5 |
| Permanent grass | 20.5 | 28.2 | 19.4 | 28.0 | 14.2 | 20.7 |
| Total area under crops and grass | 37.1 | 58.2 | 35.4 | 56.0 | 31.3 | 51.2 |
| Mountain and heathland used for grazing | 38.3 | 21.5 | 41.3 | 24.2 | 49.8 | 29.2 |

Sources: As for Tables II.1, II.2 & II.3.

**Table II.6**

RATES OF CHANGE OF THE LAND USE OF UPLAND BRITAIN,
1889-1949 (per cent)

### 1889/1919

|  | Upland England | ALL ENGLAND | Upland Wales | ALL WALES | Upland Scotland | ALL SCOTLAND | Upland Great Britain | ALL GREAT BRITAIN |
|---|---|---|---|---|---|---|---|---|
| Arable land | (−)5.5 | (−)7.1 | (−)3.8 | (−)0.9 | (−)2.1 | (−)7.2 | (−)3.8 | (−)6.8 |
| Permanent grass | (−)3.8 | (−)0.3 | (−)6.7 | (−)8.6 | (−)7.7 | 10.5 | (−)5.0 | (−)0.5 |
| Total area under crops and grass | (−)4.4 | (−)3.7 | (−)5.8 | (−)6.1 | (−)3.2 | (−)2.8 | (−)4.5 | (−)3.8 |
| Mountain and heathland used for grazing | 25.9 | 46.3 | 48.6 | 46.7 | (−)0.7 | 2.3 | 7.9 | 12.6 |

### 1919/1949

|  | Upland England | ALL ENGLAND | Upland Wales | ALL WALES | Upland Scotland | ALL SCOTLAND | Upland Great Britain | ALL GREAT BRITAIN |
|---|---|---|---|---|---|---|---|---|
| Arable land | 17.6 | 12.7 | 12.1 | 18.6 | (−)5.7 | (−)5.3 | 6.9 | 9.1 |
| Permanent grass | (−)29.9 | (−)29.1 | (−)25.4 | (−)16.7 | (−)6.9 | (−)11.5 | (−)26.8 | (−)26.2 |
| Total area under crops and grass | (−)13.3 | (−)9.3 | (−)13.3 | (−)4.9 | (−)5.9 | (−)7.1 | (−)11.6 | (−)8.6 |
| Mountain and heathland used for grazing | 25.1 | 34.8 | 25.5 | 32.7 | 18.5 | 15.4 | 20.5 | 21.1 |

Sources: Tables II.1, II.2 and II.3.

Table II.7

## THE AREA OF FOREST AND WOODLAND IN UPLAND BRITAIN, 1845-1949 (Acres)

|  | 1845 | 1881 | 1924[1] | 1947-1949[2] |
|---|---|---|---|---|
| Upland England | — | 246 434 | 282 383 | 344 603 |
| ALL ENGLAND | — | 1 466 038 | 1 630 987 | 1 865 046 |
| Upland Wales | — | 127 266 | 168 288 | 228 420 |
| ALL WALES | — | 162 786 | 253 461 | 316 478 |
| Upland Scotland | 353 540 | 549 891 | 707 453 | 895 912 |
| ALL SCOTLAND | 594 679 | 829 476 | 1 074 224 | 1 266 838 |
| Upland Great Britain | — | 923 591 | 1 158 124 | 1 468 935 |
| ALL GREAT BRITAIN | — | 2 458 300 | 2 958 672 | 3 448 362 |

1   In 1924, of the total area of forest and woodland, 2 720 000 acres (91.9%) belonged to private individuals, 40 000 acres (1.4%) to corporate bodies and 199 000 acres (6.7%) to the State.

2   In 1947-1949, of the total area of forest and woodland, 2 825 331 acres (81.9%) belonged to private individuals and 623 031 acres (18.1%) to the State.

Sources: Anderson (1967); Board of Agriculture (1883); Forestry Commission (1928); Forestry Commission (1952).

Table II.8

## THE OWNERSHIP STRUCTURE OF FOREST AND WOODLAND IN UPLAND BRITAIN, 1947-1949 (Acres)

|  | Private | State | Total |
|---|---|---|---|
| Upland England | 274 105 | 70 498 | 344 603 |
| ALL ENGLAND | 1 577 115 | 287 931 | 1 865 046 |
| Upland Wales | 159 375 | 69 045 | 228 420 |
| ALL WALES | 224 208 | 92 270 | 316 478 |
| Upland Scotland | 709 124 | 186 788 | 895 912 |
| ALL SCOTLAND | 1 024 008 | 242 830 | 1 266 838 |
| Upland Great Britain | 1 142 604 | 326 331 | 1 468 935 |
| ALL GREAT BRITAIN | 2 825 331 | 623 031 | 3 448 362 |

Source: Forestry Commission (1952).

Table II.9

THE AREA OF FOREST AND WOODLAND IN UPLAND BRITAIN AS A
PROPORTION OF TOTAL LAND AREA, 1845-1949 (per cent)

|  | 1845 | 1881 | 1924 | 1947-49 |
|---|---|---|---|---|
| Upland England | — | 3.4 | 3.9 | 4.8 |
| ALL ENGLAND | — | 4.5 | 5.1 | 5.8 |
| Upland Wales | — | 3.6 | 4.6 | 6.2 |
| ALL WALES | — | 3.2 | 5.0 | 6.2 |
| Upland Scotland | 2.7 | 4.2 | 5.6 | 7.1 |
| ALL SCOTLAND | 3.1 | 4.3 | 5.6 | 6.6 |
| Upland Great Britain | — | 4.0 | 4.9 | 6.3 |
| ALL GREAT BRITAIN | — | 4.3 | 5.3 | 6.1 |

Source: Anderson (1967); Board of Agriculture (1883); Forestry Commission (1928);
Forestry Commission (1952).

Table II.10

THE GROWTH IN FOREST AND WOODLAND AREA IN UPLAND BRITAIN,
1845-1949 (per cent)

|  | 1845/1881 | 1881/1924 | 1924/1947-49 |
|---|---|---|---|
| Upland England | — | 14.6 | 22.0 |
| ALL ENGLAND | — | 11.3 | 14.4 |
| Upland Wales | — | 32.2 | 35.7 |
| ALL WALES | — | 55.7 | 24.9 |
| Upland Scotland | 55.5 | 28.7 | 26.6 |
| ALL SCOTLAND | 39.5 | 29.5 | 17.9 |
| Upland Great Britain | — | 25.4 | 26.8 |
| ALL GREAT BRITAIN | — | 20.4 | 16.6 |

Source: Table II.7

**Table II.11**
THE AREA AND NUMBER OF DEER FORESTS IN SCOTLAND,
1790-1948 (Acres)

|  | Area | Number of Deer Forests |
|------|-----------|------------------------|
| 1790 | — | 9 |
| 1838 | — | 45 |
| 1883 | 1 975 209 | 99 |
| 1896 | 2 500 000 | 120 |
| 1912 | 3 584 916 | 203 |
| 1920 | 3 432 385 | 189 |
| 1938 | 3 349 131 | 194 |
| 1948 | 3 187 686 | 196 |

Sources: Various, cited in Darling (1955) and Bryden & Houston (1976).

**Figure 1**
ACRES OF TILLAGE PER 100 ACRES OF CROPS AND GRASS IN 1875

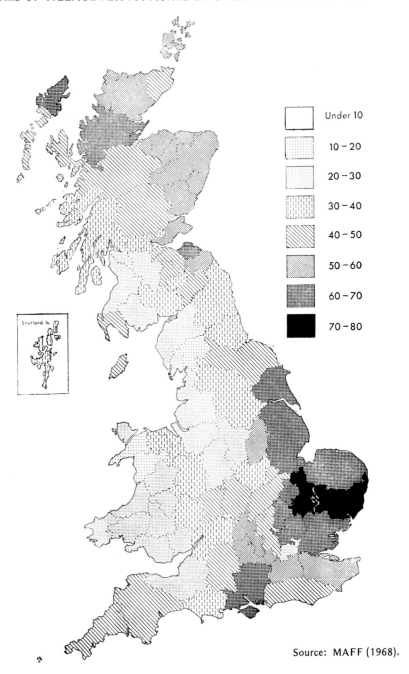

| | |
|---|---|
| | Under 10 |
| | 10 – 20 |
| | 20 – 30 |
| | 30 – 40 |
| | 40 – 50 |
| | 50 – 60 |
| | 60 – 70 |
| | 70 – 80 |

Shetland Is.

Source: MAFF (1968).

**Figure 2**
ACRES OF TILLAGE PER 100 ACRES OF CROPS AND GRASS IN 1938

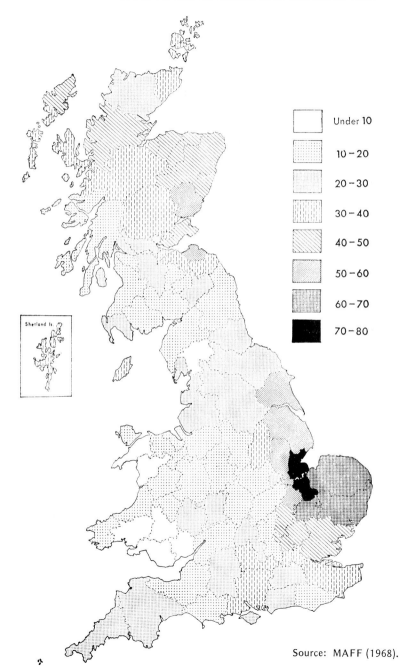

Under 10

10 – 20

20 – 30

30 – 40

40 – 50

50 – 60

60 – 70

70 – 80

Source: MAFF (1968).

**Figure 3**
ACRES OF GRASS FOR MOWING PER 100 ACRES OF CROPS AND GRASS
IN 1875

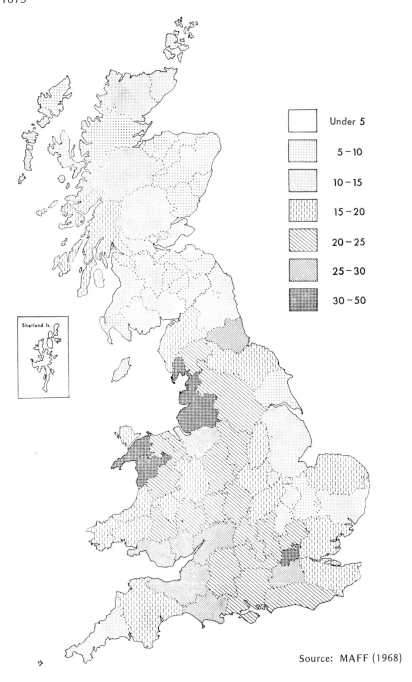

| | |
|---|---|
| | Under 5 |
| | 5 − 10 |
| | 10 − 15 |
| | 15 − 20 |
| | 20 − 25 |
| | 25 − 30 |
| | 30 − 50 |

Shetland Is.

Source: MAFF (1968)

# Figure 4
## ACRES OF GRASS FOR MOWING PER 100 ACRES OF CROPS AND GRASS IN 1938

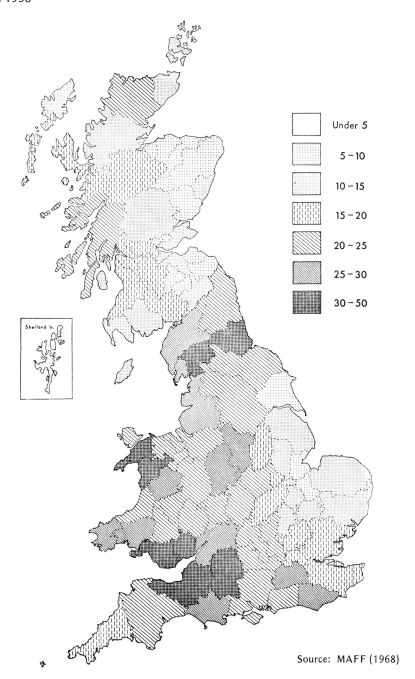

Under 5

5 – 10

10 – 15

15 – 20

20 – 25

25 – 30

30 – 50

Shetland Is.

Source: MAFF (1968)

Figure 5
PROGRESS OF THE FORESTRY COMMISSION'S ACQUISITION OF FOREST
UNITS, 1924/1929

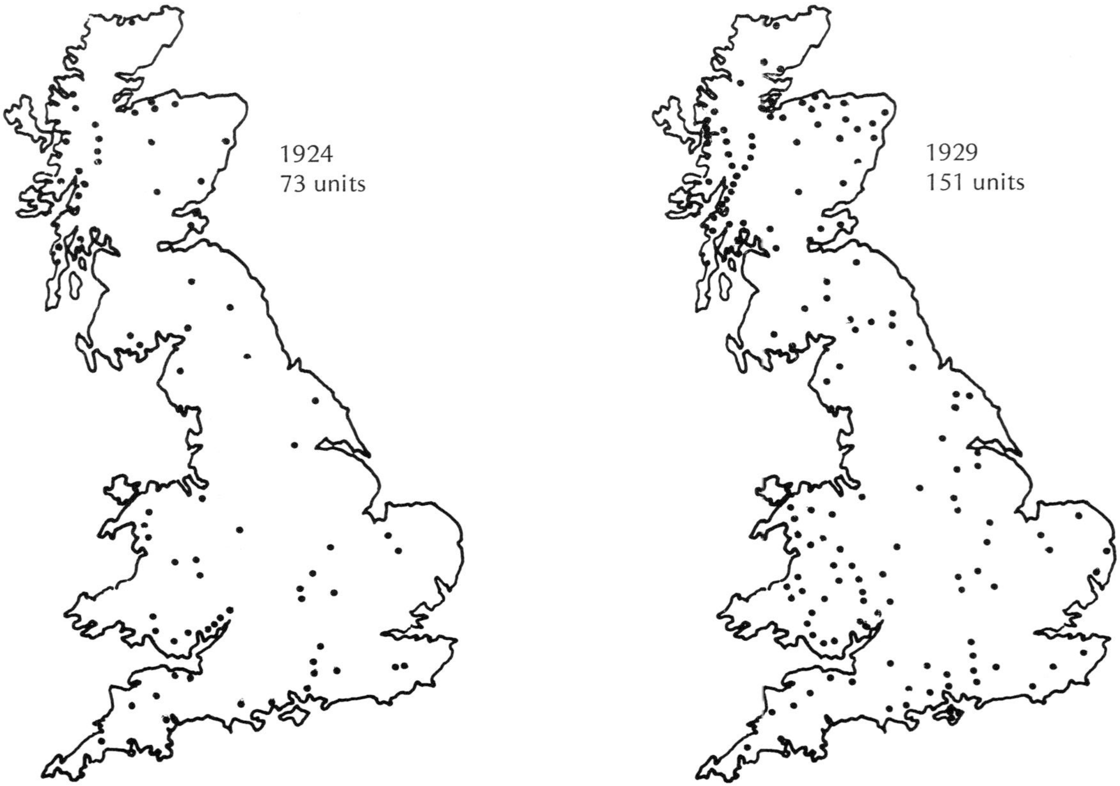

1924
73 units

1929
151 units

**Figure 6**
PROGRESS OF THE FORESTRY COMMISSION'S ACQUISITION OF FOREST
UNITS, 1934/1949

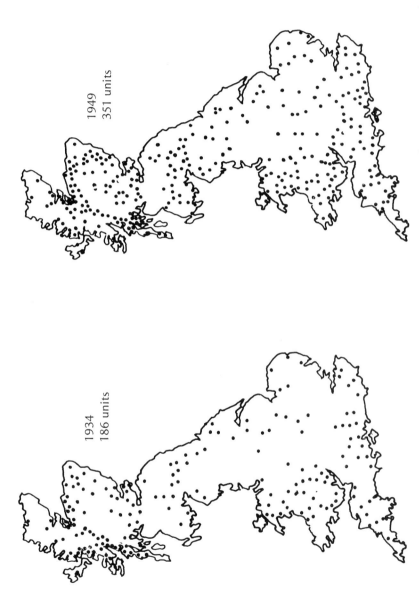

1934
186 units

1949
351 units

Source: Forestry Commission (1949)

91

Appendix III: The livestock population of upland Britain, 1800-1950

Table III.1
THE LIVESTOCK POPULATION OF UPLAND BRITAIN, 1889

| | Horses used for agricultural purposes | Total horses | Cows and heifers in milk or in calf | Total cattle | Ewes for breeding | Total sheep | Total pigs |
|---|---|---|---|---|---|---|---|
| Upland England | 118 148 | 181 117 | 351 765 | 888 829 | — | 3 438 349 | 226 045 |
| ALL ENGLAND | 764 013 | 1 091 041 | 1 752 187 | 4 352 657 | — | 15 839 882 | 2 118 385 |
| Upland Wales | 54 626 | 103 814 | 200 758 | 486 666 | — | 2 399 928 | 177 134 |
| ALL WALES | 75 227 | 141 143 | 272 031 | 666 101 | — | 2 840 689 | 240 741 |
| Upland Scotland | 71 272 | 95 427 | 172 864 | 533 755 | — | 3 389 158 | 52 137 |
| ALL SCOTLAND | 142 513 | 189 205 | 409 421 | 1 120 797 | — | 6 951 449 | 151 677 |
| Upland Great Britain | 244 046 | 380 358 | 725 387 | 1 909 250 | — | 9 227 435 | 455 316 |
| ALL GREAT BRITAIN | 981 753 | 1 421 389 | 2 433 639 | 6 139 555 | — | 25 632 020 | 2 510 803 |

Source: Board of Agriculture (1889).

**Table III.2**
THE LIVESTOCK POPULATION OF UPLAND BRITAIN, 1919

| | Horses used for agricultural purposes | Total horses | Cows and heifers in milk or in calf | Total cattle | Ewes for breeding | Total sheep | Total pigs |
|---|---|---|---|---|---|---|---|
| Upland England | 123 920 | 217 085 | 426 211 | 1 094 990 | 1 397 684 | 3 558 819 | 207 074 |
| ALL ENGLAND | 728 509 | 1 223 613 | 2 248 107 | 5 389 462 | 4 367 770 | 11 899 549 | 1 627 242 |
| Upland Wales | 62 338 | 119 551 | 227 750 | 592 730 | 1 187 152 | 2 768 679 | 126 262 |
| ALL WALES | 85 689 | 163 211 | 305 376 | 805 077 | 1 396 530 | 3 224 764 | 171 226 |
| Upland Scotland | 70 244 | 95 945 | 176 014 | 553 979 | 1 310 591 | 2 885 313 | 38 574 |
| ALL SCOTLAND | 140 617 | 189 349 | 455 625 | 1 229 637 | 2 826 123 | 6 410 039 | 137 905 |
| Upland Great Britain | 256 502 | 432 581 | 829 975 | 2 241 699 | 3 895 427 | 9 212 811 | 371 910 |
| ALL GREAT BRITAIN | 954 815 | 1 576 173 | 3 009 108 | 7 424 176 | 8 590 423 | 2 534 352 | 1 936 373 |

Sources: Board of Agriculture for Scotland (1920); Ministry of Agriculture and Fisheries (1920).

Table III.3
THE LIVESTOCK POPULATION OF UPLAND BRITAIN, 1949

| | Horses used for agricultural purposes | Total horses | Cows and heifers in milk or in calf | Total cattle | Ewes for breeding | Total sheep | Total pigs |
|---|---|---|---|---|---|---|---|
| Upland England | 63 751 | 85 431 | 629 549 | 1 421 400 | 1 249 630 | 3 247 193 | 276 023 |
| ALL ENGLAND | 286 579 | 399 752 | 3 138 150 | 6 709 513 | 2 983 913 | 8 102 377 | 1 998 843 |
| Upland Wales | 32 258 | 47 259 | 322 873 | 673 870 | 1 201 447 | 2 996 223 | 83 573 |
| ALL WALES | 48 429 | 70 583 | 465 050 | 985 381 | 1 475 846 | 3 642 062 | 132 859 |
| Upland Scotland | 31 137 | 41 162 | 209 865 | 655 066 | 1 526 702 | 3 471 084 | 60 661 |
| ALL SCOTLAND | 65 667 | 86 699 | 621 850 | 1 568 570 | 3 013 725 | 7 102 873 | 232 445 |
| Upland Great Britain | 127 146 | 173 852 | 1 162 287 | 2 750 336 | 3 977 779 | 9 714 500 | 420 257 |
| ALL GREAT BRITAIN | 400 675 | 557 034 | 4 225 050 | 9 263 464 | 7 473 484 | 18 847 312 | 2 364 147 |

Sources: Ministry of Agriculture and Fisheries (1952); Department of Agriculture for Scotland (1952).

**Table III.4**
THE LIVESTOCK POPULATION OF UPLAND BRITAIN, 1889, 1919 and 1949

| | 1889 | | 1919 | | 1949 | |
|---|---|---|---|---|---|---|
| | Upland Great Britain | ALL GREAT BRITAIN | Upland Great Britain | ALL GREAT BRITAIN | Upland Great Britain | ALL GREAT BRITAIN |
| Horses used for agricultural purposes | 244 046 | 981 753 | 256 502 | 954 815 | 127 146 | 400 675 |
| TOTAL HORSES | 380 358 | 1 421 389 | 432 581 | 1 576 173 | 173 852 | 557 034 |
| Cows and heifers in milk or in calf | 725 387 | 2 433 639 | 829 975 | 3 009 108 | 1 162 287 | 4 225 050 |
| TOTAL CATTLE | 1 909 250 | 6 139 555 | 2 241 699 | 7 424 176 | 2 750 336 | 9 263 464 |
| Ewes for breeding | — | — | 3 895 427 | 8 590 423 | 3 977 779 | 7 473 484 |
| TOTAL SHEEP | 9 227 435 | 25 632 020 | 9 212 811 | 21 534 352 | 9 714 500 | 18 847 312 |
| TOTAL PIGS | 455 316 | 2 510 803 | 371 910 | 1 936 373 | 420 257 | 2 364 147 |

Sources: Tables III.1, III.2 & III.3.

## Table III.5
## RATES OF CHANGE OF THE LIVESTOCK POPULATION OF UPLAND BRITAIN, 1889-1949 (per cent)

| | 1889/1919 | | | | | | | |
|---|---|---|---|---|---|---|---|---|
| | Upland England | ALL ENGLAND | Upland Wales | ALL WALES | Upland Scotland | ALL SCOTLAND | Upland Great Britain | ALL GREAT BRITAIN |
| Horses used for agricultural purposes | 4.9 | (−)4.6 | 14.1 | 13.9 | (−)1.4 | (−)1.3 | 5.1 | (−)2.7 |
| TOTAL HORSES | 19.9 | 12.2 | 15.2 | 15.6 | 0.5 | 0.1 | 13.7 | 10.9 |
| Cows and heifers in milk or in calf | 21.2 | 28.3 | 13.4 | 12.3 | 1.8 | 11.3 | 14.4 | 23.6 |
| TOTAL CATTLE | 23.2 | 23.8 | 21.8 | 20.9 | 3.8 | 9.7 | 17.4 | 20.9 |
| Ewes for breeding | — | — | — | — | — | — | — | — |
| TOTAL SHEEP | 3.5 | (−)24.9 | 15.4 | 13.5 | (−)14.8 | (−)7.8 | (−)0.2 | (−)16.0 |
| TOTAL PIGS | (−)8.4 | (−)23.2 | (−)28.7 | (−)28.9 | (−)26.0 | (−)9.1 | (−)18.3 | (−)22.9 |

| | 1919/1949 | | | | | | | |
|---|---|---|---|---|---|---|---|---|
| | Upland England | ALL ENGLAND | Upland Wales | ALL WALES | Upland Scotland | ALL SCOTLAND | Upland Great Britain | ALL GREAT BRITAIN |
| Horses used for agricultural purposes | (−)48.6 | (−)60.7 | (−)48.3 | (−)43.5 | (−)55.7 | (−)55.3 | (−)50.4 | (−)58.0 |
| TOTAL HORSES | (−)60.6 | (−)67.7 | (−)60.5 | (−)56.8 | (−)57.1 | (−)54.2 | (−)59.8 | (−)64.7 |
| Cows and heifers in milk or in calf | 47.7 | 39.6 | 41.8 | 52.3 | 19.2 | 36.5 | 40.0 | 40.4 |
| TOTAL CATTLE | 29.8 | 24.4 | 13.7 | 22.4 | 18.2 | 27.6 | 22.7 | 24.8 |
| Ewes for breeding | (−)10.6 | (−)31.7 | 1.2 | 5.7 | 16.5 | 6.6 | 2.1 | (−)13.0 |
| TOTAL SHEEP | (−)8.8 | (−)31.9 | 8.2 | 12.9 | 20.3 | 10.8 | 5.4 | (−)12.5 |
| TOTAL PIGS | 33.3 | 22.8 | (−)33.8 | (−)22.4 | 57.3 | 68.6 | 13.0 | 22.1 |

Sources: Tables III.1, III.2 & III.3.

**Table III.6**

CATTLE AND SHEEP POPULATIONS IN SCOTLAND, 1800-1949

| | 1800 | 1878 | 1889 | 1919 | 1949 |
|---|---|---|---|---|---|
| Crofting Counties[1]: | | | | | |
| Cows and heifers in milk or in calf | – | 90 182 | 91 262 | 89 137 | 102 180 |
| TOTAL CATTLE | 356 400 | 231 824 | 228 473 | 230 870 | 247 098 |
| Ewes for breeding | – | – | – | 938 254 | 1 110 450 |
| TOTAL SHEEP | 641 300 | 2 549 429 | 2 395 024 | 2 033 986 | 2 462 115 |
| Scotland: | | | | | |
| Cows and heifers in milk or in calf | – | 388 002 | 409 421 | 455 625 | 621 850 |
| TOTAL CATTLE | 1 047 142 | 1 095 387 | 1 120 797 | 1 229 637 | 1 568 570 |
| Ewes for breeding | – | – | – | 2 826 123 | 3 013 725 |
| TOTAL SHEEP | 2 851 867 | 7 036 396 | 6 951 449 | 6 410 039 | 7 102 873 |

1 Orkney, Shetland, Sutherland, Caithness, Ross and Cromarty, Inverness.

Sources: Sinclair (1814); Board of Agriculture (1878 & 1889); Board of Agriculture for Scotland (1920); Ministry of Agriculture and Fisheries (1920 & 1952); Department of Agriculture for Scotland (1952).

**Figure 7**
THE NUMBER OF CATTLE PER 1000 ACRES OF AGRICULTURAL LAND
(INCLUDING COMMON ROUGH GRAZING) IN 1875

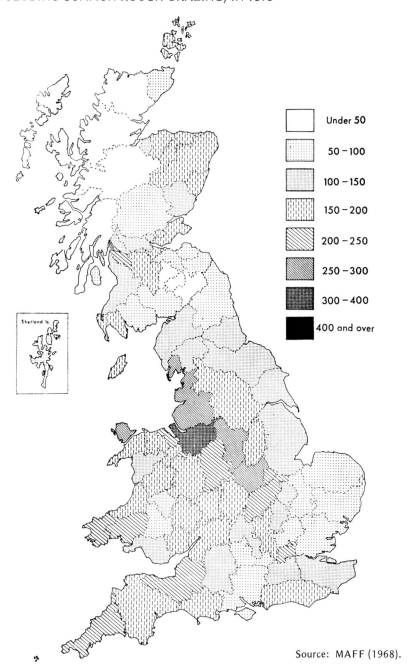

| | |
|---|---|
| | Under 50 |
| | 50 – 100 |
| | 100 – 150 |
| | 150 – 200 |
| | 200 – 250 |
| | 250 – 300 |
| | 300 – 400 |
| | 400 and over |

Shetland Is.

Source: MAFF (1968).

## Figure 8
THE NUMBER OF CATTLE PER 1000 ACRES OF AGRICULTURAL LAND
(INCLUDING COMMON ROUGH GRAZING) IN 1938

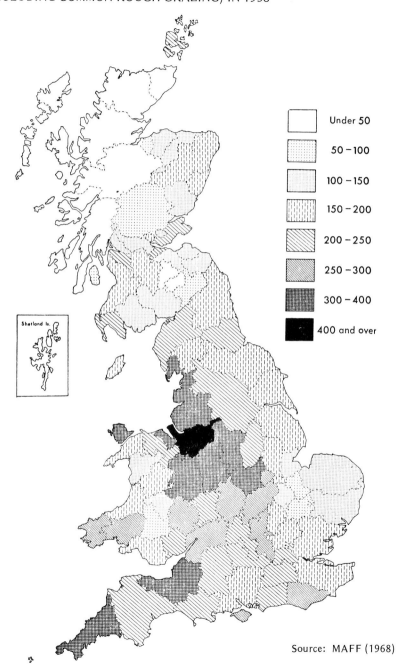

Under 50

50 – 100

100 – 150

150 – 200

200 – 250

250 – 300

300 – 400

400 and over

Shetland Is.

Source: MAFF (1968)

**Figure 9**
THE NUMBER OF SHEEP PER 1000 ACRES OF AGRICULTURAL LAND
(INCLUDING COMMON ROUGH GRAZING) IN 1875

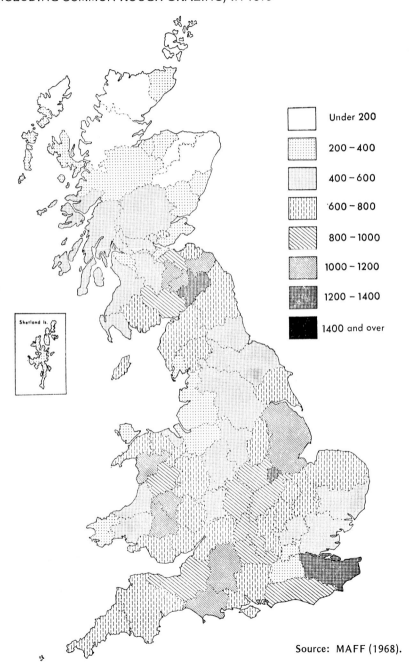

Under 200

200 – 400

400 – 600

600 – 800

800 – 1000

1000 – 1200

1200 – 1400

1400 and over

Shetland Is.

Source:  MAFF (1968).

# Figure 10
## THE NUMBER OF SHEEP PER 1000 ACRES OF AGRICULTURAL LAND (INCLUDING COMMON ROUGH GRAZING) IN 1938

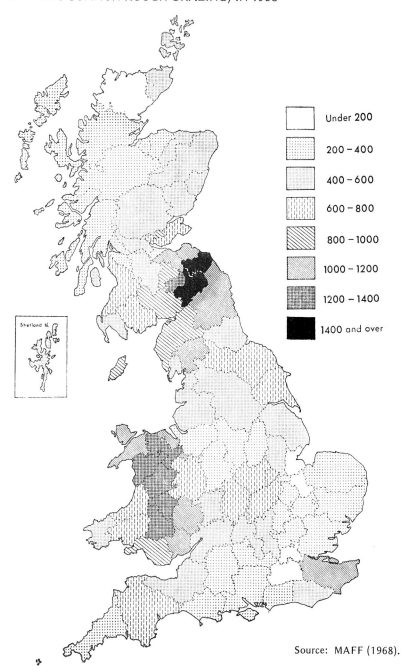

Under 200

200 – 400

400 – 600

600 – 800

800 – 1000

1000 – 1200

1200 – 1400

1400 and over

Shetland Is.

Source: MAFF (1968).

Appendix IV: Crop yields in upland Britain, 1892-1901 and 1939-1948

Table IV.1
AVERAGE CROP YIELDS[1] IN UPLAND BRITAIN FOR THE TEN YEARS, 1892-1901

| | Wheat cwt/acre | Barley cwt/acre | Oats cwt/acre | Potatoes tons/acre | Turnips and swedes (for stock) tons/acre | Hay from temporary grass cwt/acre | Hay from permanent grass cwt/acre |
|---|---|---|---|---|---|---|---|
| Upland England | 16.2 | 16.8 | 14.1 | 5.9 | 13.4 | 32.0 | 25.1 |
| ALL ENGLAND | 16.5 | 15.6 | 14.2 | 6.0 | 11.9 | 26.7 | 21.7 |
| Upland Wales | 13.1 | 13.7 | 10.9 | 6.0 | 15.2 | 22.1 | 17.3 |
| ALL WALES | 13.4 | 14.5 | 11.7 | 5.7 | 14.8 | 22.6 | 17.5 |
| Upland Scotland | 20.8 | 16.4 | 12.1 | 5.0 | 14.0 | 25.9 | 22.5 |
| ALL SCOTLAND | 20.6 | 17.2 | 13.0 | 5.7 | 15.0 | 31.7 | 28.7 |
| Upland Great Britain | 15.6 | 16.1 | 12.6 | 5.6 | 13.9 | 27.6 | 22.8 |
| ALL GREAT BRITAIN | 16.5 | 15.7 | 13.6 | 5.9 | 12.8 | 27.3 | 21.5 |

1  Ten-year weighted averages.

Sources:  Board of Agriculture (1903); MAFF (1968).

**Table IV.2**
AVERAGE CROP YIELDS[1] IN UPLAND BRITAIN FOR THE TEN YEARS, 1939-1948

| | Wheat cwt/acre | Barley cwt/acre | Oats cwt/acre | Potatoes tons/acre | Turnips and swedes (for stock) tons/acre | Hay from temporary grass cwt/acre | Hay from permanent grass cwt/acre |
|---|---|---|---|---|---|---|---|
| Upland England | 18.6 | 17.6 | 17.0 | 6.6 | 15.1 | 29.6 | 18.9 |
| ALL ENGLAND | 18.8 | 17.6 | 17.0 | 7.1 | 12.6 | 27.7 | 19.4 |
| Upland Wales | 17.2 | 14.4 | 14.0 | 5.8 | 12.1 | 20.7 | 17.0 |
| ALL WALES | 16.9 | 14.6 | 14.4 | 5.9 | 12.0 | 22.1 | 17.5 |
| Upland Scotland | 21.9 | 18.4 | 15.9 | 6.5 | 16.2 | 26.3 | 20.0 |
| ALL SCOTLAND | 21.9 | 19.6 | 16.3 | 7.2 | 17.1 | 31.4 | 28.9 |
| Upland Great Britain | 18.6 | 17.5 | 16.0 | 6.5 | 15.5 | 26.6 | 18.3 |
| ALL GREAT BRITAIN | 18.9 | 17.7 | 16.5 | 7.1 | 14.5 | 27.9 | 19.5 |

1, Ten-year weighted averages.

Sources: Ministry of Agriculture and Fisheries, Department of Agriculture for Scotland and Department of Agriculture for Northern Ireland (1952); Department of Agriculture for Scotland (1952); Ministry of Agriculture and Fisheries (1952).

Table IV.3
LONG TERM CROP YIELD CHANGES IN UPLAND BRITAIN, 1892-1901 to 1939-1948 (per cent)

| | Upland England | ALL ENGLAND | Upland Wales | ALL WALES | Upland Scotland | ALL SCOTLAND | Upland Great Britain | ALL GREAT BRITAIN |
|---|---|---|---|---|---|---|---|---|
| Wheat | 14.8 | 13.9 | 31.3 | 26.1 | 5.3 | 6.3 | 19.2 | 14.5 |
| Barley | 4.8 | 12.8 | 5.1 | 0.7 | 12.2 | 14.0 | 8.7 | 12.7 |
| Oats | 20.6 | 19.7 | 28.4 | 23.1 | 31.4 | 25.4 | 27.0 | 21.3 |
| Potatoes | 11.9 | 18.3 | (−)3.3 | 3.5 | 30.0 | 26.3 | 16.1 | 20.3 |
| Turnips and swedes (for stock) | 12.7 | 5.9 | (−)20.4 | (−)18.9 | 15.7 | 14.0 | 11.5 | 13.3 |
| Hay from temporary grass | (−)7.5 | 3.7 | (−)6.3 | (−)2.2 | 1.5 | (−)0.9 | (−)3.6 | 2.2 |
| Hay from permanent grass | (−)24.7 | (−)10.6 | (−)1.7 | 0.0 | (−)11.1 | 0.7 | (−)19.7 | (−)9.3 |

Sources: Tables IV.1 & IV.2.

# Appendix V: Mineral deposits in upland Britain

## Figure 11
## GOLD DEPOSITS IN UPLAND BRITAIN

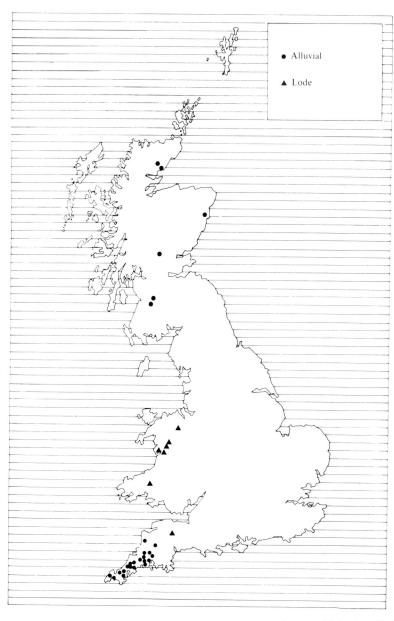

Source: Richardson (1974)

**Figure 12**
SILVER DEPOSITS IN UPLAND BRITAIN

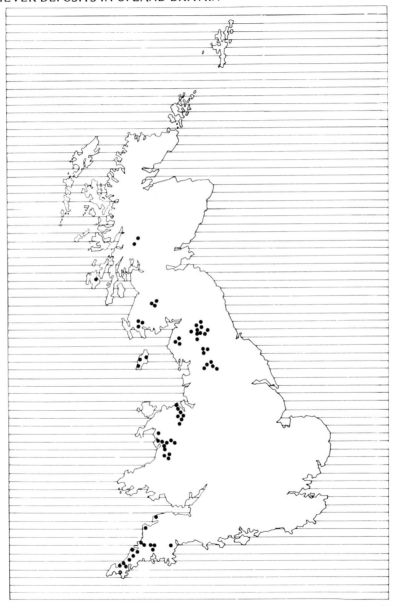

Source: Richardson (1974)

**Figure 13**
COPPER DEPOSITS IN UPLAND BRITAIN

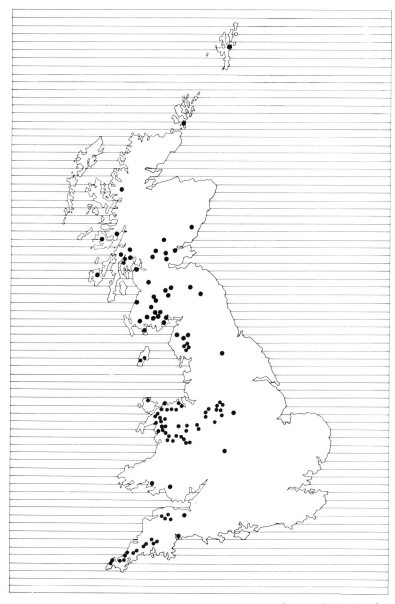

Source: Richardson (1974)

**Figure 14**
LEAD DEPOSITS IN UPLAND BRITAIN

Source: Richardson (1974)

**Figure 15**
ZINC DEPOSITS IN UPLAND BRITAIN

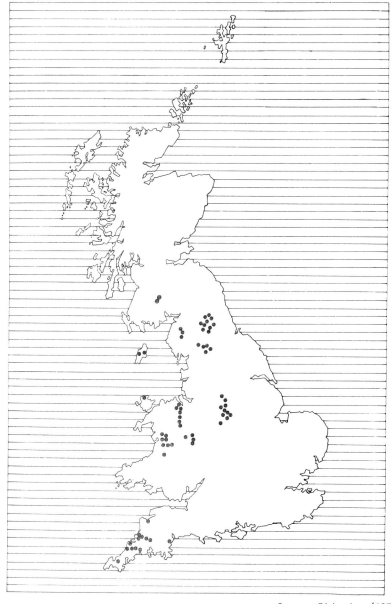

Source: Richardson (1974)

**Figure 16**
## ASSOCIATED MINERAL DEPOSITS IN UPLAND BRITAIN

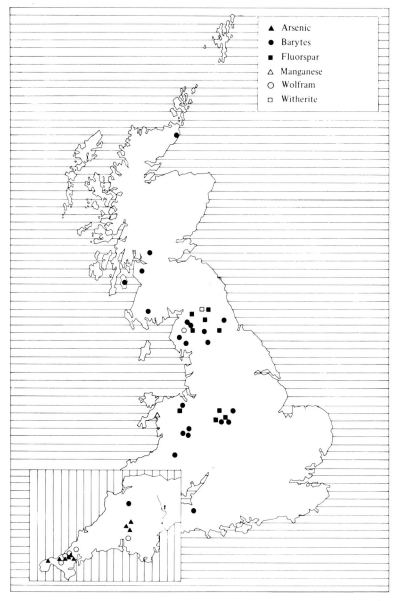

Source: Richardson (1974)

110

## ACKNOWLEDGEMENTS

Thanks are due to Mr R G Keen of the National Museum of Wales, Cardiff; Mr E Scourfield of the Welsh Folk Museum, Cardiff; and to Mr A Fenton and staff of the National Museum of Antiquities of Scotland, Edinburgh, for their assistance in finding material. I would also like to thank Mr C A Jewell of the Museum of English Rural Life and members of staff of the Department of Agriculture and Horticulture, University of Reading, for all their help in many different ways.

Figures 1, 2, 3, 4, 7, 8, 9 and 10 are taken from *A century of agricultural statistics, Great Britain, 1866-1966,* and are reproduced with the permission of the Controller of Her Majesty's Stationery Office; Figures 5 and 6 are reproduced with the permission of the Forestry Commission from their *29th Annual Report;* and Figures 11, 12, 13, 14, 15 and 16 are reprinted by permission of Penguin Books Ltd from *Metal Mining* by J B Richardson (Allen Lane, 1974) pages 14, 33, 77, 108, 153 and 162, Copyright © J B Richardson, 1974.

# REFERENCES AND SELECT BIBLIOGRAPHY

Anderson, M L (1967)   *A history of Scottish forestry, Volume 2.*   Edinburgh: Nelson.

Ashby, A W & Evans, I L (1944)   *The agriculture of Wales and Monmouthshire.*   University of Wales Press.

Astor, Viscount & Rowntree, B S (1938)   *British agriculture: the principles of future policy.*   London: Longmans Green.

Attwood, E A & Evans, H G (1961)   *The economics of hill farming.*   University of Wales Press.

Bell, M (Ed.) (1975)   *Britain's National Parks.*   Newton Abbot: David & Charles.

Berridge, N G (1969)   *A summary of the mineral resources of the Crofter Counties of Scotland.*   National Environmental Research Council.   London: HMSO.

Board of Agriculture (1878)   *Agricultural returns of Great Britain, 1878.*   London: HMSO.

Board of Agriculture (1883)   *Agricultural returns of Great Britain, 1883.*   London: HMSO.

Board of Agriculture (1889)   *Agricultural returns of Great Britain, 1889.*   London: HMSO.

Board of Agriculture (1892)   *Agricultural returns of Great Britain, 1892.*   London: HMSO.

Board of Agriculture (1903)   *Agricultural Statistics, Great Britain, 1902.*   London: HMSO.

Board of Agriculture for Scotland (1914)   *Report on the home industries in the Highlands and Islands.*   Edinburgh: HMSO.

Board of Agriculture for Scotland (1920)   *Agricultural statistics, 1919, Scotland, Part I.*   Edinburgh: HMSO.

Bouch, C M L & Jones, G P (1961)   *A short economic history of the Lake Counties, 1500-1830.*   Manchester University Press.

Bowley, M (1960)   *Innovations in building materials.*   London: Duckworth.

Bremner, D (1869)   *The industries of Scotland.*   New reprinted edition, 1969.   Newton Abbot: David & Charles.

British Association (1963)   *The north-east of Scotland.*   Aberdeen: Central Press.

British Parliamentary Papers (1801-1951)   *Great Britain Census.*   London: HMSO.

British Parliamentary Papers (1802-1803)   *Survey and reports of the coasts and central highlands of Scotland, Volume 4.*   London: HMSO.

Bryden, J M & Houston, G F B (1976)   *Agrarian change in the Scottish Highlands.*   London: Martin Robertson and HIDB.

Butt, J (1967)   *Industrial archaeology of Scotland.*   Newton Abbot: David & Charles.

Caird, J (1852)   *English agriculture in 1850-51.*   London: Longman Brown.

Cairncross, A K (Ed.) (1954)   *A statistical account of Scottish life: The Scottish economy.*   Cambridge University Press.

Campbell, R H & Dow, J B A (1968)   *Source book of Scottish economic and social history.*   Oxford University Press.

Carr, H R C & Lister, G A (1948)   *The mountains of Snowdonia.*   London: Lockwood.

Clapham, J H (1963)   *An economic history of modern Britain: machines and national rivalries.*   New Edition. Cambridge University Press.

Collier, A (1953)   *The crofting problem.*   Cambridge University Press.

Darling, F F (1955)   *West Highland Survey: an essay in human ecology.*   Oxford University Press.

Defoe, D (1962 edition)   *A tour through the whole island of Great Britain.*   Everyman edition in two volumes.   London: Dent.

Department of Agriculture for Scotland (1952)   *Agricultural statistics, 1945-49, Scotland, Part I.*   Edinburgh: HMSO.

Department of Agriculture for Scotland (1954)   *Report of the commission of enquiry into crofting conditions.*   Edinburgh: HMSO.

Dodd, A H (1971)   *The industrial revolution in North Wales.*   University of Wales Press.

Edlin, H L (1956)   *Trees, woods and man.*   London: Collins.

Forestry Commission (1920-1950)   *Annual Reports.*   London: HMSO.

Forestry Commission (1928)   *Report on census of woodlands, 1924.*   London: Forestry Commission.

Forestry Commission (1952)   *Census of woodlands, 1947-1949.*   London: Forestry Commission.

Franklin, J B (1952)   *A history of Scottish farming.*   London: Nelson.

Geological Survey (1940)   *Special reports on the mineral resources of Great Britain, Volume 33.*   London: HMSO.

Gibbon, J M (1933)   Scottish goldfields and their story.   *Scottish Bankers Magazine.*

Gray, M (1957)   *The Highland economy, 1750-1850.*   Edinburgh: Oliver & Boyd.

Gregor, M J F & Crichton, R M (1946)   *From croft to factory.*   London: Nelson.

Gulvin, C (1973)   *The tweedmakers.*   Newton Abbot: David & Charles.

Hall, A D (1913)   *A pilgrimage of British farming, 1910-1912.*   London: John Murray.

Howell, J P (1922)   *The productivity of hill farming.*   Oxford: Agricultural Economics Research Institute.

Howse, W H (1952)   *Old time Llandrindod.*   Llandrindod.

Hunter, R (1933)   *The water supply of Glasgow.*   Glasgow.

Jenkins, J G (1969)   *The Welsh woollen industry.*   Cardiff: National Museum of Wales.

Jenkins, J G (1971)   Commercial salmon fishing in Welsh Rivers.   *Folk Life,* **9,** 29-60.

Jennings, B (1967)   *A history of Nidderdale.*   Huddersfield: Advertiser Press.

Jennings, B (1970)   *A history of Harrogate and Knaresborough.*   Huddersfield: Advertiser Press.

Jones, A (1927)   *The rural industries of England and Wales, Volume 4.*   Oxford: Clarendon Press.

Jones, J G (1969-1972)   The Ffestiniog slate industry: the industrial pattern 1831-1913.   *Journal of the Merioneth Historical and Record Society,* **6.**

de Lauvergne, L (1855)   *The rural economy of England, Scotland and Ireland.*   London.

Lewis, W J (1967)   *Lead mining in Wales.*   University of Wales Press.

Lickorish, L J & Kershaw, A G (1958)   *The travel trade.*   London: Practical Press.

Lindsay, J M (1975)   Charcoal iron smelting and its fuel supply, the example of Lorn Furnace, Argyllshire, 1753-1876.   *Journal of Historical Geography,* **1,** 283-298.

Lythe, S G E & Butt, J (1975)   *An economic history of Scotland, 1100-1939.*   Glasgow: Blackie.

MAFF (1968)   *A century of agricultural statistics, Great Britain, 1866-1966.*   London: HMSO.

Malthus, T (1798)   *Essay on population.*   London.

Marshall, J D (1958)   *Furness in the Industrial Revolution.*   Barrow: Barrow Public Library.

Maxton, J P (Ed.) (1936)   *Regional types of British agriculture.*   London: Allen & Unwin.

Miles, R (1967)   *Forestry in the English landscape.*   London: Faber & Faber.

Ministry of Agriculture and Fisheries (1920)   *Agricultural statistics, 1919, England and Wales, Part I.*   London: HMSO.

Ministry of Agriculture and Fisheries (1952)   *Agricultural statistics, 1945-49, England and Wales, Part I.*   London: HMSO.

Ministry of Agriculture and Fisheries, Department of Agriculture for Scotland and Department of Agriculture for Northern Ireland (1952)   *Agricultural statistics, 1948-49, United Kingdom, Part I.*   London: HMSO.

Mitchell, B R (1962)    *Abstract of British historical statistics.*    Cambridge University Press.

Moisley, H A (1961)    Harris tweed: a growing Highland industry.    *Economic Geography,* **37**, 353-370.

Morrison, T A (1975)    *Goldmining in western Merioneth.*    Llandysal.

North, F J (1962)    *Mining of metals in Wales.*    Cardiff: National Museum of Wales.

Oakley, C A (1937)    *Scottish industry today.*    Edinburgh: Moray Press.

O'Dell, A C & Walton, K (1962)    *The Highlands and Islands of Scotland.* London: Nelson.

Orwin, C S & Sellick, R J (1972)    *The reclamation of Exmoor Forest.*    New Edition. Newton Abbot: David & Charles.

Pearsall, W H (1950)    *Mountains and moorlands.*    London: Collins.

Porteous, J M (1876)    *God's Treasure House in Scotland.*    Edinburgh.

Pryde, G S (1962)    *Scotland from 1603 to the present day.*    London: Nelson.

Raistrick, A (1967)    *Old Yorkshire Dales.*    Newton Abbot: David & Charles.

Rees, D M (1973)    *The metalliferrous mines of Wales.*    Cardiff: National Museum of Wales.

Richardson, J B (1974)    *Metal mining.*    London: Allen Lane.

Rollinson, W (1967)    *A history of man in the Lake District.*    London: Dent.

Scottish Development Department (1967)    *The Cairngorm area.*    Edinburgh: HMSO.

Scott Watson, J A & Hobbs, M E (1951)    *Great farmers.*    London: Faber & Faber.

Select Committee on Forestry Education (1887)    *Report.*    London: HMSO.

Sinclair, J (Ed.) (1814)    *General report of the agricultural state and political circumstances of Scotland.*    5 volumes. Edinburgh.

Spence, C C (1960)    *God speed the plough.*    University of Illinois Press.

Stamp, L D & Beaver, S H (1935)    *The British Isles: a geographic and economic survey.*    London: Longmans.

Stapledon, R G (1936)    *A survey of the agricultural and waste lands of Wales.* London: Faber & Faber.

Stapledon, R G (1946)    The hill lands of England and Wales.    *Agriculture,* **53**, 99-101.

Symon, J A (1959)    *Scottish farming past and present.*    Edinburgh: Oliver & Boyd.

Trevelyan, G M (1949)    *An autobiography and other essays.*    London: Longmans Green.

Turnock, D (1974)    *Scotland's Highlands and Islands.*    Oxford University Press.

Welsh Agricultural Lands Sub-Commission (1955)   *Report of mid Wales investigation.*   London: HMSO.

Zimmermann, E W (1933)   *World resources and industries.*   New York: Harper.